I0818365

interbeing

Also by Thich Nhat Hanh

Anger
The Art of Communicating
The Art of Living
The Art of Power
At Home in the World
Awakening of the Heart
Be Free Where You Are
Being Peace
Beyond the Self
The Blooming of a Lotus
Breathe, You Are Alive!
Call Me by My True Names
Chanting from the Heart
Creating True Peace
Cultivating the Mind of Love
The Diamond That Cuts through Illusion
The Dragon Prince
Fear
Fragrant Palm Leaves
Friends on the Path
The Heart of the Buddha's Teaching
Hermitage among the Clouds
How to See
Joyfully Together
Living Buddha, Living Christ
Love in Action
Love Letter to the Earth
Master Tang Hoi
The Mindfulness Survival Kit
The Miracle of Mindfulness
No Death, No Fear
No Mud, No Lotus
Old Path White Clouds
Our Appointment with Life
Peace Is Every Step
Present Moment Wonderful Moment
Reconciliation
Stepping into Freedom
The Stone Boy
The Sun My Heart
Teachings on Love
Thundering Silence
Touching Peace
Transformation and Healing
Two Treasures
Understanding Our Mind
The World We Have

THICH NHAT HANH

THE 14 MINDFULNESS TRAININGS
OF ENGAGED BUDDHISM

4TH EDITION

BERKELEY, CA

Parallax Press
PO Box 7355
Berkeley, CA 94707
parallax.org

Parallax Press is the publishing division of
Plum Village Community of Engaged Buddhism, Inc.

Cover design by Katie Eberle
Text design by Debbie Berne
Calligraphy by Thich Nhat Hanh
Image courtesy of Lion's Roar
Author photo © Plum Village Community of Engaged Buddhism

Non-English words are in Sanskrit unless otherwise indicated or
made clear by the context.

Printed in Canada by Friesens

Parallax Press's authorized representative in the EU and the EEA is
SAS PLUM VILLAGE AT HOME- Point UH
437 Chemin du Pey, Thenac, France
Email: europe@parallax.org

This hardcover edition ISBN: 978-1-967175-25-3
Paperback ISBN: 978-1-946764-20-1
Ebook ISBN:978-1-946764-19-5

Library of Congress Cataloging-in-Publication Data is available upon request.

1 2 3 4 5 FRIESENS 30 29 28 27 26

Spiritual practice is the basis
for all social action.

Contents

Part Three
The Charter of the Order of Interbeing

Part Four
Ceremonies

Foreword to the Fourth Edition

Sister Chân Không

As a young person, I was deeply impressed by the teachings of the Buddha Śākyamuni. This led me to intensify my work helping hungry children in the slums of Saigon, and to make the decision to leave behind my boyfriend of five years to become a Buddhist nun. But when I visited nunneries in Saigon, Bến Tre, and other places, the nuns told me to practice well so I could be reborn as a man and become a Buddha. I knew this was a misunderstanding of the teachings of the Buddha. I didn't want to be reborn as a man in order to become enlightened. I didn't even care about being enlightened. I only cared about helping hungry children, poor people, and suppressed people. I decided to set up my own nunnery. When I was able to meet Thầy, I asked him about what I had been told by the nuns. Thầy smiled, saying that is an old-fashioned way to interpret Buddhism: during the time the Buddha was alive there were many women who were enlightened during the practice. One day a nun gave a beautiful Dharma talk on the functioning of our mind, which her former husband heard. He then asked the Buddha, "Is the teaching given by my former wife correct?" The Buddha answered: "The Buddha would have said the same if asked to give a teaching on the functioning of our mind."

Rather than agreeing that I become a nun, Thầy offered me and others of his students the Fourteen Mindfulness Trainings. When I read these trainings, I was overwhelmed with joy, thinking that Thầy had devised them especially for the young people of my generation. I did not realize, as Thầy later told me, that they were an expression of the deepest teachings of the Buddha taken from the Avataṃsaka Sūtra, Diamond Sutra, and the Lotus Sutra, etc. Thầy explained that the Buddhism being practiced at that time was too outdated and he wanted to renew not just the teachings but also the practice. He had asked his teacher in the root temple in Huế if he could have a new Dharma name: One (Nhất) Action (Hạnh), which suited his aspiration to renew Buddhism.

He then left the Buddhist Institute in Huế, in order to fulfill his ideal of renewing Buddhism; this was in the late 1940s. In 1950, he wrote his first book, a slim volume on Buddhist logic.

In 1958 I enrolled in the University of Saigon to study biology. But what really inspired me was working in the slums. I found a poor area of Saigon only five blocks from the university. Every noon break, I would run to the slum, spend a few hours there, and then run back to school. I would sit and listen to people talk about their hardships and think of ways to help them. I continued my university studies only to please my parents and the kind and excellent professor who was my mentor.

One project I started was giving "rice scholarships" to orphans and children of single parents. The parents depended on their children to earn a little money selling newspapers or sweets. I knew that well-to-do people rarely thought of the poor, so I began planting seeds of generosity in them, asking them to set aside a handful of rice each day for poor children. I helped set up a daycare center in the slum, facilitated obtaining birth certificates for children so they could enroll in school, and taught those who weren't able to go to school. I helped some of the parents get small loans to start a business, and transported sick people to the hospital on my motorbike. I later discovered that this is called "social work," but at the time, I didn't know I was a social worker.

In October, 1959 Thầy Mãn Giác gave me a book by Thích Nhất Hạnh. I learned that in December Thầy would begin teaching a three-month course at Xá Lợi Temple in Saigon, so I enrolled. The first lecture I heard him give impressed me deeply. I had never heard anyone speak so beautifully and profoundly. It was the fifteenth of November, 1959.

Thầy felt that Buddhism had much to contribute to real social change. He wanted to find ways to support a movement for social change according to the Buddhist spirit. He said he would help my friends and me with our social projects.

I knew Thầy was the teacher I had been looking for. Inspired by his teachings and encouragement, I attracted seventy friends to join me in caring for five slums around Saigon. We took medicine and food to those who were ill, held night classes for adults, and taught children about the great men and women of Vietnam.

In February 1961 Thầy offered another three-month course. An atmosphere of sisterhood and brotherhood began to develop among Thầy and his students. In April, he began another weekly course on Buddhism for twenty of us university students. Thầy moved to Trúc Lâm Temple, a one-hour motorbike ride from Saigon, and taught the course there.

From May to September 1961, I went with a dozen friends every Saturday to study with Thầy at the Trúc Lâm Temple, and we stayed until late in the evening. Then we rode back to Saigon, singing together under the moonlight. These were wonderful days. We loved and respected each other dearly, like thirteen brothers and sisters. Learning from Thầy, we became the "thirteen cedars" of the Buddhist movement in South Vietnam. Thầy wanted to continue his efforts to renew Buddhism by training a number of young people to become "like strong cedars to help support the Buddha's teachings."

We thirteen cedars decided to apply our Buddhist understanding by setting up a night school for poor workers, soldiers, and working teenagers. We realized we were becoming a happy Sangha, a community of practice, helping others. In September Thầy told us that he had accepted a fellowship to study comparative religion at Princeton University. He was in the US for two years. I continued my social work and my university studies.

In April 1960, Thầy had started the Buddhist Student Union. I was head of the social welfare branch. We held weekly meetings to study Buddhism, discuss the Dharma, plan projects for the poor, and publish a magazine describing our work. The thirteen cedars became eighty, and then there were over 300 cedars in the Buddhist Student Union.

In December 1963, Thầy returned to Vietnam, when the Catholic US-backed Diệm Regime had just been overthrown. In January 1964, Thầy submitted a Three-Point Proposal to the Executive Council of the Unified Buddhist Church in Vietnam, saying the United Buddhist Congregation must:

1. publicly call for the cessation of hostilities in Vietnam, South and North.
2. help build an Institute for the study and application of Buddhism.
3. develop a center for training social workers to help bring about nonviolent social change based on the Buddha's teachings.

Thầy's idealism appealed to university students, and many volunteered to help with all three of his projects. The Institute of Higher Buddhist Studies opened in February 1964. Young volunteers staffed the office. The program was fully underway in just fourteen months, when its name was changed to Vạn Hạnh University.

Thầy's idea about social work was that it should go beyond traditional notions of charity, supporting the peasants in their own efforts to improve the quality of their lives. Thầy saw social work and rural development as the work of

Thích Nhất Hạnh in 1965.

personal and social transformation, with workers and peasants seeing each other not as "helpers" and "those being helped," but as partners in a common task.

In February 1964, Thầy set up a pioneer village on the outskirts of Saigon. I was in France finishing my studies when he wrote to me, "Please come back right away. If you want to work for social change in the ways we spoke about, this is the time. Many people want to help, but you are the one person who can organize this program and make it work."

I finished my thesis and returned to Vietnam in June 1964. I helped start a second pioneer village and spent all my days with the poor in the pioneer villages and the slums. Our goal was to train young people to help peasants establish schools and medical centers, improve sanitation, and develop agriculture and horticulture. We also did flood-relief work whenever Vietnam was hit by flooding.

In September 1965, the School of Youth for Social Service (SYSS) was founded as a program of Vạn Hạnh University, although the groundwork had begun as soon as Thầy had returned to Saigon in 1963.

By 1966, Thầy had finished compiling the Fourteen Mindfulness Trainings as part of his deep aspiration to renew Buddhism. The trainings contain the essence of the traditional Prātimokṣa (the monastic precepts) as well as the traditional lay and monastic Bodhisattva Precepts. Many Vietnamese monks and nuns who practice the traditional precepts are moved when they read the Fourteen Mindfulness Trainings. They say that these trainings speak to them deeply and water the seeds of the mind of love (*bodhicitta*) in them.

The Fourteen Trainings I received in 1966 along with five other members of the SYSS were the first draft Thầy prepared before again departing for the US, this time to call for peace at the invitation of Cornell University. He compiled the Fourteen Trainings as a matter of urgency before his imminent departure. He thought that there would be another transmission of the Fourteen Trainings for more students of the School of Youth for Social Service when he returned from the US, but as a result of his calling for peace, he was exiled for forty years, and it wasn't until 2005 that the next transmission of the Fourteen Trainings in Vietnam could take place.

There were six of us who were the first to receive the Fourteen Trainings. They were three women: myself, Cao Ngọc Phương, Sister Phan Thi Mai, and Sister Phạm Thúy Uyên; and three men: Brother Bùi Văn Thanh, Brother Đo Văn Khon, and Brother Nguyễn Văn Phúc. At that time the three young women wanted to practice celibacy and become nuns, but the three young men already had fiancées. Thầy's wish for us was to wait until there were both men and women ready for the monastic ordination so that the Sangha would have both monks and nuns.

At the time of the ordination I was a lecturer in botany at Huế University. Phan Thi Mai (or Nhất Chi Mai) was a schoolteacher, and it was she who immolated herself in the cause of peace on May 16, 1967. (My photo appeared in the *New York Times* on May 17, 1967, announcing Mai's self-immolation.)

Sister Phạm Thúy Uyên is still alive and lives in Saigon with her widowed mother. Bùi Văn Thanh was at that time engaged to my younger sister. He was in charge of the credit loans given by the School of Youth for Social Service to poor people. We would loan them fifty US dollars, for example, so that they could raise ten pigs and develop two acres of rice fields. Meanwhile he also worked as a judge in the tribunal court of Mỹ Tho city.

Đó Văn Khon was very active in the Buddhist Youth Movement (Gia Đình Phật Tử). Three years after the war

The first six members of the Order of Interbeing (*l to r*): Phạm Thúy Uyên, Cao Ngọc Phương, and Phan Thi Mai; Nguyễn Văn Phúc, Bùi Văn Thanh, and Đó Văn Khon.

ended, he died when he was still very young. Nguyễn Văn Phúc was very dedicated in working in the Vạn Hạnh University. After the ordination, he married the woman he loved. He has also died.

The six of us were all important organizers in the School of Youth for Social Service. Thầy wanted all of the 300 trainees of the SYSS to receive the Order of Interbeing (OI) Fourteen Mindfulness Trainings, but he was exiled beginning in May 1966. After 1966, no ordinations took place until 1981. Then Thầy ordained his niece Anh-Hương. She had come to the United States with her father (the elder brother of Thầy), escaping Vietnam as boatpeople. In 1981 she visited

Thầy in Plum Village, France, and Thầy really wanted her to receive the OI training for laypeople. After hearing me recite the Fourteen Trainings, she asked if she could receive them.

Thầy knew that of the 300 students of the School of Youth for Social Service not all of them would become monks and nuns. This is why Thầy compiled the Fourteen Mindfulness Trainings to be the same for monks, nuns, and laypeople. The Fourteenth Mindfulness Training, which has separate wording for lay and monastic practitioners, was only elaborated after I shaved my head on Vulture Peak in 1988. When I received the Fourteen Mindfulness Trainings in 1966, they were a different version from the one we use today and it had fewer words.[1]

In my autobiography, I say that Plum Village grew out of Thầy's wish to have a spiritual practice center for the School of Youth for Social Service. Now it is a practice center for all activists in service for this world. When Thầy went to the West, he extended his wish to help all activists, not just those engaged in social service in Vietnam. Plum Village has become a place of practice for ecological activists, for artists, for helping professionals—those who work in hospitals or drive ambulances. They need mindfulness in order to stop, to breathe, and to smile. The OI Fourteen Trainings train people to live deeply in every aspect of their life.

During the war, those who were in the School of Youth Social Service with Thầy were very active. The first OI members did so much. The young OI members of today often have

---

[1] See Appendix, p.179.

not experienced war in their own country, but their diligence and eagerness to serve are just as strong as they were in us. Of course at that time the situation was very urgent. Because of the atrocities of war we saw being committed every day and because the suffering was so great, the Buddha nature in each of us was called up in response. The Buddha nature is equal in everyone. Nobody forced us to go out and risk our lives in service, and if you had been there, you would have acted as we did then. It was the same for Nhất Chi Mai: before she heard me describe the atrocities that were happening, she was not moved to work for peace. After she saw what was happening, she became deeply committed to working for peace and immolated herself in its cause.

The problem of our own time is that we, and especially young people, lack ethical guidelines. We need mindfulness trainings so that we do not harm ourselves and others by sexual misconduct, violent speech, and drug addiction, and so we know how to practice in order to not burn out.[2] I have heard of teenagers who threaten to kill their parents if they do not give them money to buy drugs. In Buddhism we learn that whatever we think, speak, or do has repercussions for ourself and for others. The repercussions for ourself are called the main retribution (正報) and the repercussions that create the environment in which we live are called the

[2] Not only has Thầy compiled the Fourteen Mindfulness Trainings, he has also updated the Five Precepts (Pañcaśīla) of the Buddha, in the form of the Five Mindfulness Trainings, which can be seen on pp. 146–151 and at: https://plumvillage.org/mindfulness-practice/the-5-mindfulness-trainings/

environmental retribution (依報). The environmental retribution includes our family, our society, and our country. Whether someone's actions are beautiful or not depends largely on their environmental conditions. The environment in the time of the Buddha Śākyamuni was different from the environment in which Thầy and my generation grew up, and the environment now is also different. This is why we need to update the ethical guidelines we practice in order for them to be in tune with the environment in which people are living. The Five and the Fourteen Mindfulness Trainings need to be revised every ten years or so because society is always changing, and with it, the problems that we need ethical guidelines to face. Those of you who were born twenty or forty years later than me have grown up in a very different environment from the one I grew up in. You may come from an intellectual family as I did, but the intellectual circles when I was growing up were very different from what they are now. If you look at the Eighth Mindfulness Training on True Community and Communication you will see it is very different from the first version.

I think that Thầy has been awarded peace prizes not only because he's peaceful, but also because of his contribution to making the world peaceful with the Five and the Fourteen Mindfulness Trainings. The Sixth Mindfulness Training on Taking Care of Anger has also been revised. When you are angry, you always want to fight. The Training instructs you to stop and to look deeper. Instead of going in the direction your anger is leading you, you are able to stop with mindful breathing and walking, and when you are calmer, you see another side to the matter, you are less aggressive, and you achieve what you really want to change in a peaceful way. If the whole of humanity tried to practice just the Five Mindfulness Trainings, we would have a wonderful world, without needing the Fourteen Mindfulness Trainings. However we are very fortunate to have the Fourteen Trainings as well because they help us to go deeper and deeper into the teachings and the practice.

The first step is always to receive and practice the Five Mindfulness Trainings. Before requesting to become an aspirant to receive the Fourteen Mindfulness Trainings, you have to practice the Five Trainings for at least two years in order to prove that you are really active, that you really love the practice, and implement it in a concrete and valuable way.

As a monk, Thầy has practiced the 250 Bhikshu Precepts as well as the major and minor Bodhisattva Precepts. When he compiled the Fourteen Mindfulness Trainings, he was continuing the ancestral teachers who in the past had compiled the Bodhisattva Precepts that are found in the Brahmajāla Sūtra. The Fourteen Mindfulness Trainings are a Bodhisattva Vow that are more appropriate to our time.

I want to encourage everyone, whether you are Christian, Jewish, Hindu, or Muslim, or whatever your religious or political beliefs might be, to train yourself in the direction of beauty, depth, and great love. Your own tradition has its own precepts, ethics, and wisdom that lead to understanding and love. When there is great understanding and love, you can call it God in you, or you can call it the Buddha nature in you. Nevertheless, developing great love demands training, and the Fourteen Mindfulness Trainings instruct us all, Buddhist and non-Buddhist, how to train that great love in ourselves. The word "training" is more suitable than the word "precepts" because it helps us to see that we are training to go in a certain direction.

Hue, Vietnam
August, 2019

Introduction
Fred Eppsteiner

The Order of Interbeing (Tiếp Hiện) was formed by Thích Nhất Hạnh in the mid-1960s, shortly before he was exiled from Vietnam and at a time when the Vietnam War was escalating and the teachings of the Buddha were desperately needed to combat the hatred and violence that was dividing his country. On the full moon day of February 1966, Zen Master Thích Nhất Hạnh ordained six members into the Order, three men and three women ranging in age from twenty-two to thirty-two. All of them were founding members of the School of Youth for Social Service, which he had helped establish the year before.

From its inception, the Order of Interbeing was comprised of all the four groups of the original Buddhist community (Sangha)—monks, nuns, laymen, and laywomen. Of the first six ordinees, the three women chose to live celibate lives like nuns, although they did not shave their heads or take all the formal vows of Buddhist nuns, and the three men chose to marry and practice as lay Buddhists.

The ordination was a wonderful celebration. Each ordinee was presented with a lamp with a handmade shade on which Thích Nhất Hạnh had calligraphed Chinese characters like "Lamp of Wisdom," "Lamp of the Full Moon," and "Lamp of the World." During the ceremony, the six ordinees vowed to study, practice, and observe the Fourteen Mindfulness Trainings of the Order of Interbeing, a wonderful blend of traditional Buddhist morality and contemporary social concerns.

Forged in the crucible of war and devastation, these guidelines helped the first six brothers and sisters, who were doing war relief work and helping to rebuild bombed villages, cultivate serenity, understanding, and compassion even in the midst of the tragedy of war. Though they continued to stay busy helping war victims, organizing demonstrations, printing books and leaflets, running social service projects, and organizing an underground network to help draft resisters, they renewed themselves with a Day of Mindfulness each weekend. "I so looked forward to these days," recalls Sister Chân Không. "I dwelled mindfully on each act, starting with the way I put down my overnight bag in my room, boiled water to prepare a bath, and then put on my meditation clothes. First I did walking meditation alone in the woods and picked some wildflowers and bamboo branches for flower arrangements. Then, after a few hours of dwelling mindfully in each act and releasing most of my worries, I began to feel renewed." After practicing sitting and walking meditation, the six members gathered together to recite the Fourteen Mindfulness Trainings and chant the Heart of the Prajñāpāramitā Sūtra.

For ten years, no new members were permitted to join the Order's core community. In fact, this "period of experimentation" was extended until 1981, when Anh-Hương

Nguyễn, niece of Thích Nhất Hạnh, a microbiologist and lay meditation teacher, living in Virginia, USA became the seventh member of the Order. Today, there are more than two thousand members of the core community and many thousands more worldwide who recite the Fourteen Mindfulness Trainings regularly. *The Mindfulness Bell,* a journal of the art of mindful living, inspired by the teaching of Thích Nhất Hạnh lists hundreds of Sanghas around the globe, groups of people in local communities who come together to study, practice, and discuss the Fourteen Mindfulness Trainings.

In 1992, the Order of Interbeing held its first International Council in Plum Village. Various committees were set up to take care of different aspects of the life and teachings of the Order. The second International Council, called "Being Wonderfully Together," was held in Plum Village in September 1996 and was attended by more than one hundred core community members from four continents. An Executive Council was formed, and the Order's structure and activities were thoroughly reviewed. This fourth edition of the book *Interbeing* includes the 2012 revised version of the Fourteen Mindfulness Trainings of the Order of Interbeing, relevant commentary, and the Order's Charter, last revised in 1996–1997. The Order is continuing to take shape as a true expression of the bodhisattva practice of socially Engaged Buddhism.

The Fourteen Mindfulness Trainings of the Order of Interbeing remain uniquely applicable to contemporary moral dilemmas. The Order was formed at a time when destruction in the name of supposedly irreconcilable "isms" was painfully evident in Vietnam. Thích Nhất Hạnh was acutely aware of the need for all people to overcome ideological divisiveness, and, accordingly, the first three trainings directly reject fanaticism and political or religious self-righteousness.

The Fourth goes to the heart of Buddhist compassion and directs a challenge to all practitioners: contemplative reflection on the suffering of living beings is not enough; we must help diminish suffering through compassionate involvement and this means first and foremost being in touch with and understanding our own suffering. This training suggests that the only way to end suffering is to understand the causes of suffering. This is the teaching of the Four Noble Truths.

The Fifth Mindfulness Training is about consumption. Without mindful consumption we cannot be happy and compassionate people. We need to look deeply into what kinds of nutriments we consume, whether edible food and drink, sense impressions, or consciousness.

The Sixth Training encourages us to take care of our anger as soon as it arises—taking care of it rather than suppressing it, denying it, or being carried away by it—and then looking deeply into its roots in our own consciousness.

The Seventh Training, at the core of all fourteen, shows us how mindfulness, awareness, and returning to the breath are the keys to maintaining peace and happiness in everything we do.

The Eighth, Ninth, and Tenth Trainings address communication, loving speech, Sangha building, and harmony in our community, issues as pressing today as in the war-torn environment in which they were forged. They provide a model of Right Thinking, Speech, and Action, never losing sight of the need to speak out about social injustice and oppression from the all-embracing, nonpartisan viewpoint that has been taught by the Buddha.

The Eleventh Mindfulness training shows how Right Livelihood is important not just for the human species but for the very survival of our planet.

The traditional Buddhist admonition against killing is described in the Twelfth Mindfulness Training, which enjoins us to respect and not destroy life, nor to support any act of killing in our thinking and in our way of life.

And does not the Thirteenth Training on non-stealing speak to the fact that the well-stocked shelves of one country relate directly to the empty shelves of another, that profit-making at the cost of human suffering and the suffering of other living beings is an ethical concern.

The final Mindfulness Training deals with the suffering that is brought about by irresponsible sexual behavior and teaches us to take care of our sexual energy so that we do not harm ourselves and others out of sexual desire. It reminds us that respecting life and committing ourselves to ending suffering is as real an issue within the area of sexual relationships as in the political and social arenas.

The Fourteen Mindfulness Trainings of the Order of Interbeing are guidelines for anyone wishing to live mindfully. By developing peace and serenity through ethical and mindful living, we can help our society make the transition from one based on greed and consumerism to one in which thoughtfulness and compassionate action are of the deepest value. The Fourteen Mindfulness Trainings of the Order of Interbeing embody the deepest teachings of the Buddha on Right View and the other aspects of the Noble Eightfold Path. They are a contribution to a global spirituality and ethic. In Buddhism, as in all the great world religions, the embodiment of ethical guidelines and the application of mindfulness in our daily lives is what leads to a more compassionate society, one in which the sacredness of all things great and small is revealed. These teachings of Applied Mindfulness represent a beacon of hope for today's world.

Part One

The Order of Interbeing (Tiếp Hiện)

The Meaning of Tiếp Hiện

We begin this book with an explanation of the Vietnamese name that Thích Nhất Hạnh gave to the Order of Interbeing, because the essence of the Order can best be understood when we understand the meaning of its name.

In Vietnamese the Order of Interbeing is called the Tiếp Hiện Order.[1] The words Tiếp Hiện (接現) have many meanings.

Tiếp has three meanings. The first meaning of Tiếp is to receive. What do we receive? We receive goodness, beauty, insight and a sense of morality from our ancestors. From our spiritual ancestors we receive the wonderful Dharma, the teachings that lead to insight and awakening. Therefore the first thing a member of the Order of Interbeing needs to do is to be able to receive the good and beautiful qualities that our ancestors have handed on to us. For example, as you watch your teacher or any brother or sister, who is stable in their practice, invite the bell with mindfulness and concentration, you can learn the way to invite the bell from them. Whether

---

[1] See Part Three: The Community of Interbeing and the Order Member, p. 203.

you are a monk, a nun, or a lay order member, you can learn a great deal from a stable practitioner. When you observe them closely, with your full attention, transmission happens very quickly. The way that he or she walks, stands, and interacts is their way of transmitting to us. All we need to do is to observe and we shall receive.

We receive from the Buddha, from our ancestral teachers, from our teacher and our fellow brothers and sisters who are practicing diligently. Sometimes people who are younger than we are may be able to embody the transmission better than we do, so we can also receive and learn from them. We receive an inheritance, not of money or jewels, but of the right Dharma. We can all ask ourselves: How much of my inheritance have I received? Our ancestral teachers are very eager to hand on to us this precious inheritance but are we ready or able to receive it? Learning and practicing the Dharma is a process of receiving. When we put into practice what we have received, we reap the benefits right away; we are nourished by our inheritance.

The second meaning of Tiếp is to continue, as in tying two strings together to make a longer string. It means extending and perpetuating the career of enlightenment that began with the Buddha and has been continuing ever since. We continue the Buddha, the ancestral teachers, our own teacher of this lifetime, and our blood ancestors. Someone who has filial piety is someone who continues to fulfil the deep aspirations of their ancestors. A student who has loyalty to his teacher is someone who is able to continue the calling of his teacher. If we want to continue our teacher then we have to receive his or her aspirations and practice to realize them.

The third meaning of Tiếp is to be in touch. To begin with we are in touch with the wonderful present moment, the miracle of life that is present in us and around us. If we want to be in touch, we have to come out of our shell and look clearly and deeply at the wonders of life—the snowflakes, the moonlight, the beautiful flowers—but we also need to recognize the suffering that exists—fear, anxiety, hunger, disease, and oppression. If we are not in touch with all this, we are not truly alive. When we are in touch with life, we are nourished, we transform and grow. So to be in touch means to be in touch with the suffering within our self as well as the suffering in our environment, our family, and society. Once we have truly understood this suffering, we will know what to do to transform it, as well as what we should not do. Being in touch with the suffering helps us to understand and love ourselves and others better, and helps us to transform.

Many people distinguish between the inner world of our mind and the external world around us. But these worlds are not separate; they belong to the same reality. The ideas of inside and outside, internal and external are helpful in everyday life, but they can become obstacles that prevent us from experiencing the ultimate reality. If we look deeply into our mind, we see the world deeply at the same time. If we understand the world, we understand our mind. This is called "the unity of mind and world."

Modern Christianity speaks in terms of vertical and horizontal theology whereby the vertical axis represents our spiritual relation to God and the horizontal axis represents our relation to other human beings. In Buddhism, we also think in these terms, but in Buddhism the vertical and horizontal dimensions are one. If we penetrate the horizontal, we find the vertical, and vice versa. If we touch the vertical dimension deeply, we discover the horizontal. This is the true meaning of "being in touch."

The second part of the Order's name, Hiện 現, has four meanings. First of all it means the present moment. What we touch in the present moment is life itself. We touch the Pure Land or the Kingdom of God. Sometimes the word is translated as 見, which means to see what is happening around us. The only moment of life available to us is the present moment. It is the only moment that is real. The peace we desire is not in some distant future, but it is something we can realize right in the present moment. To practice Buddhism does not mean to endure hardship now for the sake of happiness, peace, and liberation in the future. The purpose of practice is not to be reborn in some paradise or Buddha land after death. The purpose is to touch peace and happiness for ourselves and others right now, while we are alive and breathing. Means and ends cannot be separated. As practitioners we care about the means, because we see that cause and effect are one. An enlightened person will not say, "This is only a means to an end." While sitting, walking, cleaning, working, or serving, we should feel peace within ourselves. The aim of sitting meditation is to enjoy sitting, to be peaceful and fully alive during sitting meditation. Working to help the hungry or the sick means to be peaceful, loving, and compassionate while doing so. When we practice, we do not expect the practice to pay large rewards in the future, we do not expect to attain nirvana, the Pure Land, enlightenment, or Buddhahood. The secret of Buddhism is to be awake here and now. There is no way to peace; peace is the way. There is no way to enlightenment; enlightenment is the way. There is no way to liberation; liberation is the way.

The second meaning of Hiện is that which is happening in the present moment (as in *hiện pháp*, 現法). This can also be translated as 見法, that which we are able to see happening in the present moment. What we see is the pine tree swaying in the storm, the lightning, the clouds, and the rain but we can also recognize the Sangha body embracing us. These are all things with which we can be in touch. We need to see and be in touch with the suffering taking place in the world. We do not remain in our ivory tower, in our reasoning, or our ideology. We have to touch reality deeply and experience the wonders of reality. Only when we are able to be in touch with what is really happening can we realize the practice of *dṛṣṭa-dharma-sukha-vihāra* "dwelling happily in the present moment." This is the

Dharma door of living peacefully and joyfully every moment.

The third meaning of Hiện is to make our objectives become real (as in *thực hiện,* 實現). Ideas about understanding and compassion are not enough. Understanding and compassion must be real in our lives. They must be seen, touched, and felt. The real presence of understanding and compassion in our lives will alleviate suffering and give rise to joy. This transformation creates harmony between ourselves and nature, between our own joy and the joy of others. Once we get in touch with the source of understanding and compassion, our actions will naturally protect life and not cause harm.

If we wish to share joy and happiness with others, we must have joy and happiness within ourselves. If we wish to share calmness and serenity, we should first realize them within ourselves. Without a calm and peaceful mind, our actions will only create more trouble and destruction in the world.

The ripening or realization of our practice is thực hiện. Our aspiration is to realize freedom. We know that true happiness can only be realized when we have freedom. We want to wrench ourselves free from the net of attachment, hatred, or jealousy that is imprisoning us.

There is a very short sutra in the Saṃyutta Nikāya in which a god, on observing how wandering monks and nuns travelled freely, praised them for not being caught in nets of attachment with the following verse:

Like deer who have escaped from the trap
Running freely in the four directions
The monk disciples of the Buddha
Are free and at ease like that.

Monks and nuns practice to be like such deer who are able to avoid being trapped, running and jumping freely. This sutra tells us that a number of monks were residing in a forest for the Rains' Retreat. Every day they practiced sitting meditation, walking meditation, Dharma sharing, eating mindfully in silence, and they enjoyed great happiness for the entire three-month retreat.[2] Also living in that forest were a number of gods who felt very happy to be able to profit from the presence of the monks. At the end of the three months, all the monks went off to travel the countryside and the forest became deserted. On realizing the monks had left, one of the gods felt extremely sad and wept. The other gods asked him: "Why are you weeping?"

The god replied: "For the past three months, a number of monks have been on retreat here, sitting in meditation, practicing Dharma sharing and silent eating. It was so peaceful and joyful. Now they have all gone. Where have they gone?"

Another god replied: "They have gone to Kosala, Vaiśali and other places." They are free people, like deer who have

[2] Dharma sharing is a time to sit together and share with each other our joys, difficulties, and experience in the practice.

avoided the traps set for them. They can run and jump freely in the four directions. The disciples of the Buddha have that freedom and happiness.

But thực hiện, realizing our aspirations, does not mean to build a practice center. Even the European Institute of Applied Buddhism or any of our other practice centers—no matter how big or impressive—is not the most important realization. Thực hiện is the realization of the practice. The most important thing for a practitioner to realize is freedom. That is the aim, the direction a monk, nun, or layperson should go in.

As students of the Buddha, whether monastic or lay, we do not want to live a life of bondage and enslavement, and if we want freedom, we have to make an effort to practice. The value of a practitioner lies in their daily practice. That practice can liberate us from deceptive nets of status, honor, fame, profit, and sensual desire.

The fourth meaning of hiện is to adapt to modern needs (as in *hiện đại hoá*, 現代化). This means that the Dharma that we practice and teach has to be appropriate for the intended audience, in accord with the spirit of the Buddha's teachings, and suitable for the times we are living in.

With all these different meanings how could we possibly translate the words Tiếp Hiện into English? This is why, when we needed to give the Order a name in English, we gave it the name Order of Interbeing, which is a translation of a Chinese term found in the teaching of the Avataṃsaka Sūtra. If you do not know Vietnamese, it is good to become acquainted with the meaning of the words Tiếp Hiện 接現, which have origins in Chinese. If you know the meaning of these two words, you will understand the essence of the Order of Interbeing and know the nature of its practice.

With an understanding of these two Vietnamese terms we can better understand what is meant by Engaged Buddhism, the Buddhism that is engaged in the world and does not stay within the confines of the monastery. The monastery is not something cut off from life. The monastery should be looked on as the nursery garden for the planting of saplings. It is the place where we develop and preserve Dharma doors that can be practiced out in the world. Buddhism is present for the sake of the world. Buddhism is not present for the sake of Buddhism. If the world were not there, there would be no need for Buddhism. In the monastery we are protected and we have the right conditions to grow, but when we have grown we must take social action, action that helps relieve suffering in the world.

Engaged Buddhism and Applied Buddhism

In Chinese, there is no explicit term for "Engaged Buddhism" but there is an expression 人世佛教 (*rù shì fó jiào*), which means "Buddhism in the world or in society." This is the same as Engaged Buddhism. From 1930 onward, a movement was started in Vietnam to make Buddhism more relevant and responsive to people's everyday lives. At that time Buddhist magazines had just begun to write about "Buddhism in the world."

When I was still a child, at the age of about ten, I already felt the influence of this kind of Buddhism. I read magazines and books and knew that in the past Buddhism had played an important part in bringing peace and stability to my country. In my studies of history I realized how prosperous the country had been during the Lý and Trần eras, when everyone from the king to his ministers and subjects practiced Buddhism. Buddhism was the spiritual force and practice of the whole nation. The kings and ministers of the Lý and Trần dynasties mastered the practice. The first king of the Trần dynasty was Trần Thái Tông. Although as a politician he had to spend much time on matters of governance, he still managed to find time to practice meditation and short ceremonies of repentance six times daily.

At the age of twenty, the king experienced great suffering and consequently developed a strong aspiration to become a monk. It was the practice of Buddhism that helped him successfully overcome his suffering and remain a good king. He studied Buddhism extensively and practiced looking deeply in meditation. He wrote books on meditation practice that are still extant today. They include: *Forty-Three Koans for Meditation Practice,* and *Six Daily Liturgies of Repentance.* Every two hours he would stop what he was doing and practice for twenty minutes before resuming his work on affairs of state. It is highly doubtful that any of our current world leaders do anything like this. A spiritual life nourishes us and gives us the stability and insight to be a good political leader, a good head of state. We should not say: "I have too much work to do. It's not possible to practice walking meditation." If a king could practice many times a day, how can we make the excuse that we cannot practice because we have too much to do?

Engaged Buddhism did not start in 1930. It has existed from the very beginnings of the Buddhist tradition.

As well as the expression "Engaged Buddhism" we now use the term "Applied Buddhism" as in other applied disciplines, such as Applied Science, Applied Physics, and Applied Mathematics.

When we give teachings on the meaning of the Three Jewels—the Buddha, the Dharma, and the Sangha—we also have to show people how to apply these teachings in their daily lives. When we recite "I take refuge in the Buddha" (Pali: *Buddhaṃ saranaṃ gacchāmi*), these are just words, a mere proclamation, unless we know how to really take refuge. In order to truly take refuge we have to produce the energy of mindfulness, concentration, and insight. Only when we are protected by these energies can we also be protected by the energy of the Three Jewels.

We practice taking refuge in the Three Jewels with the help of the following gāthā:

Being an island unto myself
As an island unto myself
Buddha is mindfulness
Shining near, shining far.
Dharma is the breathing
Guarding body and mind.
The Sangha is the Five Skandhas
Working in harmony.

We need to train ourselves to produce the energy of mindfulness, concentration, and insight by being aware of our breathing. If we can do this, it means we have truly taken refuge in the Three Jewels and are therefore protected by them. At times when we are struggling, feeling let down, or at our wits' end, not knowing what to do next, that is when we need to come back and take refuge in the energy of the Three Jewels. Taking refuge is a practice. It is not wishful thinking, a belief, or a proclamation. When we are experiencing difficulties and have lost balance, we need to cultivate mindfulness, concentration, and insight. With this practice, we regain our stability and can see the situation more clearly, which enables us to know what to do and what not to do. That is Applied Buddhism. We apply it to our own lives to help resolve our difficulties.

However eloquently we talk about the Three Jewels, if our teachings cannot be applied, we cannot call it Applied Buddhism; it is just theoretical Buddhism. In the West there are many universities that confer PhDs in Buddhist Studies, but they are not Applied Buddhist Studies. When students of Buddhist Studies come across difficulties in their own lives and are at their wits' end, they need the kind of Buddhist Studies that can really help them.

Whatever we teach, whether the Four Noble Truths, the Noble Eightfold Path, the Five Faculties, the Five Powers, or the Seven Factors of Enlightenment, we must be able to apply it in our daily life; it should not be pure theory. We may be able to speak eloquently on the Lotus Sutra or the Avataṃsaka Sūtra. We can analyze the Diamond Sutra very skillfully, but what we say is just to satisfy the intellect. We have to ask ourselves: "How can I apply the Lotus Sutra so that it helps me when I am at my wits' end, when I am suffering or in despair? How can I apply the Diamond Sutra, the Four Noble Truths, the Noble Eightfold Path to my life? When we can answer these questions, that is Applied Buddhism. The idea of Applied Buddhism is to complement Engaged Buddhism. Buddhist Studies in Vietnam as well as in universities throughout the world tends to be very cerebral, very theoretical, but the kind of Buddhist Studies we really need is Applied Buddhist Studies. Our practice must go hand in hand with our studies. As a monastic or lay Dharma teacher, we offer Applied Buddhism to whoever comes and asks for teachings, and in our daily life we have to be an exemplar of Applied Buddhism. We only teach what we practice. We teach what we have been able to realize.

The Mindfulness Trainings

Members of the Order of Interbeing commit to observe and practice the Fourteen Mindfulness Trainings. We call them Mindfulness Trainings rather than precepts because this reminds us that they are practices, not prohibitions. They do not restrict our freedom; they protect us. They guarantee our liberty and prevent us from getting entangled in difficulties and confusion. Practicing them brings a lot of joy. We know that the trainings have not dropped from the sky but are the fruit of our own practice of mindfulness, concentration, and insight.

In the Pali Dhammapada we read:

Mind precedes all dhammas.[3] *Mind is their chief; they are all mind-made. If with a corrupted mind a person speaks or acts, suffering follows like the wheel that follows the foot of an ox.*

Mind precedes all dhammas. Mind is their chief; they are all mind-made. If with a clear mind a person speaks or acts, happiness follows like a never-departing shadow.

[3] Dhammas refers to phenomena and events, whatever we perceive.

That is the teaching of the Buddha. Mind is supreme; mind is the foundation. That is why it makes sense to present the trainings relating to the mind first, and to present the trainings on speech and the body later on.

One of the teachings of the Buddha from which the trainings have evolved is the Sutra Spoken to the King of the Ocean (Taisho number 598 in the Chinese canon; in Sanskrit: *Sāgara-nāga-rāja-pariprcchā sūtra*). In this sutra the Buddha proposed ten precepts of which three pertain to the mind: no craving, no anger, and no wrong view. There are four precepts relating to Right Speech: not lying, not causing division by saying one thing to one person and something else to another, not insulting, and not exaggerating. And there are three precepts that relate to bodily action: not killing, not stealing, and no harmful sexual behavior.

However, we need to present the Mindfulness Trainings outlined in the Sutra Spoken to the King of the Ocean in such a way that addresses the suffering of our time, so we have reformulated them to make them more relevant to today's concerns. However, it was difficult to fit everything into just ten precepts, which is why we have made them into fourteen. The Fourteen Mindfulness Trainings reflect the Eightfold Path, the essential teaching of both Theravāda and Mahāyāna Buddhism.[4] The Eightfold Path can be described as the foundation of all Buddhist training. The Eightfold Path also

---

[4] See Thich Nhat Hanh, *The Heart of the Buddha's Teaching* (Berkeley: Parallax Press, 1998); (New York: Harmony Books, 2015).

begins with the mind—Right View and Right Thought. We can arrange the Fourteen Trainings into three categories. The first seven deal with the mind, the next two with speech, and the last five with the body, although we must realize that this division is not absolute as, looking deeply, we see that each training contains all the others.

Revising the Fourteen Mindfulness Trainings

The work of revising the precepts, the trainings, took place even during the time of the Buddha. As society changes, the way of presenting the trainings should be changed also to respond to the new situation. So the new version of the Five Trainings and the Fourteen Trainings have been worked on collectively by the Sangha, and many Dharma teachers participated. So if anyone in the Sangha would like to offer some kind of insight and ideas, they are encouraged to contact Dharma teachers in their Sanghas to propose those ideas. The ideas or proposals will be recorded so that the next time when the trainings are revised, people will meditate and try taking into account that proposal. That is the way we do it as a Sangha. Because there will be revisions later on, in the course of practice.

Just as I originally tried to make the ten precepts in the Sutra Spoken to the King of the Ocean more relevant to our times, we should also revise and update the Fourteen

Mindfulness Trainings periodically. The first revision of the Fourteen Mindfulness Trainings took place in 1993, almost thirty years after their inception. A second revision was made shortly afterward in 1996, and there was a third sixteen years later in 2012. People all over the world from many different traditions highly commend the Fourteen Mindfulness Trainings and enjoy practicing them. Still, we need to keep revising them from time to time to make sure they reflect the problems we face in our society and our ever-changing world.

The latest revision of the Fourteen Mindfulness Trainings came soon after the latest revision of the Five Mindfulness Trainings, and new elements in the Five Trainings were included in the Fourteen. Both are concrete expressions of Applied Buddhist ethics. The Five Trainings are reflected in the Fourteen and the Fourteen in the Five. In 2009 the Five Mindfulness Trainings were revised for the second time. First we took the essential points from the Fourteen Mindfulness Trainings to improve the Five, and then in the revision of the Fourteen, which was completed in 2012, we took essential points from the Five to further improve the Fourteen. The present Five Mindfulness Trainings are like Bodhisattva Precepts.[5] You only need to practice the Five Mindfulness Trainings and you can become a bodhisattva. In the beginning the

[5] Bodhisattva Precepts are traditionally to complement the Bhikshu and Bhikshuni Precepts, to make them not just proscriptive but also affirmative in the direction of compassionate action. In Vietnam it is the tradition that when monks and nuns receive the full ordination, they also receive the traditional Bodhisattva Precepts. In Plum Village the monks and nuns receive the Fourteen Mindfulness Trainings as their Bodhisattva Precepts.

Fourteen Mindfulness Trainings were devised as a kind of Bodhisattva Precepts.

For a revision of the trainings to take place, a committee of senior monastic and lay practitioners will work together to make a preliminary draft revision. Once the committee has a final draft version, there should be a General Assembly of the Order to accept the revision.

During the revision process, we may need to conflate one or more Mindfulness Trainings in order to make space for a new training if the circumstances in society at that time demand it.

During the forty-five years of his ministry, the Buddha changed his way of teaching and practice greatly. The Wheel of the Dharma needs to turn a little every day. If we look at the history of Plum Village, we see that we are always making progress, always discovering new ways of teaching that are more effective. This is why we need to revise the trainings from time to time. In the field of information technology, every year there is a new kind of software. In the field of education, there are new methodologies and textbooks every year. It is the same in Buddhism; there has to be progress. The wheel of evolution has to keep turning because only then can Buddhism play its role of spiritual leadership. As Order members we know that we must take the lead in moving forward, in keeping the Dharma Wheel turning; the Buddhas and ancestral teachers expect this of us.

Part Two

Commentaries on the Fourteen Mindfulness Trainings

The Fourteen Mindfulness Trainings with Commentary[6]

The First Mindfulness Training
Openness

Aware of the suffering created by fanaticism and intolerance, we are determined not to be idolatrous about or bound to any doctrine, theory, or ideology, even Buddhist ones. We are committed to seeing the Buddhist teachings as a guiding means that help us learn to look deeply and develop our understanding and compassion. They are not doctrines to fight, kill, or die for. We understand that fanaticism in its many forms is the result of perceiving things in a dualistic or discriminative manner. We will train ourselves to look at everything with openness and the insight of interbeing in order to transform dogmatism and violence in ourselves and the world.

---

[6] This revision of the trainings was finalized in April 2012.

The Fourteen Mindfulness Trainings were born in a sea of fire in 1966 in Vietnam. The situation of the war was extremely hot. And we know how hot the fire of fanaticism can be. That is why the very first precept is about nonattachment to views, openness, and tolerance, because we see that attachment to views, narrowness, and fanaticism is the ground of a lot of suffering. As members of the core or the extended community, we know that we have to learn about and gain the insight of interbeing. We should not be dogmatic, we should not be attached to any kind of ideology or views. That is the basic teaching of the Buddha and that is the first precept of the Order of Interbeing.

The First Mindfulness Training of the Order of Interbeing reveals the openness and tolerance of Buddhism. According to Buddhism, if we do not continue to expand the boundaries of our understanding, we will be unable to go forward on the path of insight.

The Buddha's teachings are a means of helping people. They are not an end in themselves, they are not something to worship or fight over. Clinging fanatically to an ideology or a doctrine not only prevents us from learning new ways of seeing things, but also creates bloody conflicts. The worst enemies of Buddhism are fanaticism and narrow-mindedness. Religious and ideological wars have marred the landscape of human history for millennia. Holy wars have no place in Buddhism, because killing destroys everything Buddhism stands for. The destruction of lives and moral values during the Vietnam War was very much the fruit of fanaticism and narrowness. The Order of Interbeing was born during a time of utmost suffering, like a lotus flower arising from a sea of fire. Understood in this context, the First Mindfulness Training of the Order of Interbeing is the compassionate voice of the Buddha resonating in an ocean of hatred and violence.

In the spirit of interbeing, each one of the trainings contains all the others. The First Mindfulness Training includes all the others, and all the other trainings contain the first. We can see clearly that the first is the basis of the twelfth training, which urges us to protect all life. In Buddhism, actions are seen to arise in three domains: in body, speech, and mind. We usually think that killing is a physical action and occurs in the domain of the body, but a fanatical mind can cause the killing of not just one, but millions of human beings. If we were to truly follow the guidance of the First Mindfulness Training, all weapons would become obsolete.

The teachings and practices found in Buddhism may vary, but all of them aim at liberating the mind. Openness and nonattachment to views are the guiding principles for all endeavors leading to reconciliation and peace. They are also the doors that lead to the world of ultimate reality and absolute freedom.

The Buddha regarded his own teachings as a raft to cross the river and not as an absolute truth to be worshipped or clung to. Ideological inflexibility is responsible for so much of the conflict and violence in the world. Many Buddhist texts, including the Kālāma Sūtra, the Arittha Sūtra (Knowing the Better Way to Catch a Snake), and the Vajracchedikā Sūtra (The Diamond That Cuts through Illusion), address this important subject.

The first training teaches us to guard against dualistic thinking and discrimination because these attitudes lead to fanaticism, prejudice, and intolerance. When we observe the terrorism and consequent anti-terrorism in the world at this time, we see how both stem from clinging to dualistic ways of seeing others and the world—the idea that "they" are different from "us"—and the failure to see that we interare.

We need to look deeply into the nature of interbeing because all of us have the seeds of discrimination in the depths of our consciousness which need to be transformed. Those of us who practice as members of the core community or the extended community know that we have to transform this tendency of dualistic thinking.

Clinging to views can prevent us from arriving at a deeper, more profound understanding of reality. Buddhism urges us to transcend even our own knowledge if we wish to advance on the Path of Awakening. Views, *drishti* (*dṛṣṭi*), are regarded as "obstacles to knowledge."

The First Mindfulness Training of the Order of Interbeing opens us to the total openness and absolute tolerance of Buddhism. Openness and tolerance are not merely ways to deal with people in daily life; they are truly gateways for the realization of the Way. According to Buddhism, if we do not continue to expand the boundaries of our understanding, we will be imprisoned by our views and unable to realize the Way.

In our own time, in the fields of politics, sociology, psychology, ethics, and even much of science, as well as in society in general, dualistic thinking is a significant obstacle. Mind and matter are seen as two separate entities that exist independently of each other; the subject of perception (the one perceiving) is seen as being different from the object of perception (that which is being perceived). Particle physicists have now been able to see that the thing observed is not a reality separate from the observer.

The first training highlights the need for us to gain insight into the reality of nonduality, as already outlined in the first of the Five Mindfulness Trainings. With the insight of no separate self, of interbeing, and of the nondualistic nature of all that is, we are able to put an end to discrimination, prejudice, and intolerance.

When we read discourses of the Buddha, we often encounter the expression, "the great roar of the lion," which is the truth loudly and clearly proclaimed by the Buddha himself or one of his great disciples. The First Mindfulness Training of the Order of Interbeing is one such roar of the lion: the compassionate voice of the Buddha admonishing us not to be caught in any ideology or system of thought whatsoever.

The Second Mindfulness Training
Nonattachment to Views

Aware of the suffering created by attachment to views and wrong perceptions, we are determined to avoid being narrow-minded and bound to present views. We are committed to learning and practicing nonattachment to views and being open to others' experiences and insights in order to benefit from the collective wisdom. Insight is revealed through the practice of compassionate listening, deep looking, and letting go of notions rather than through the accumulation of intellectual knowledge. We are aware that the knowledge we presently possess is not changeless, absolute truth. Truth is found in life and we will observe life within and around us in every moment, ready to learn throughout our lives.

The Second Mindfulness Training is born from and is closely linked to the First and also deals with the mind. This training warns us not to get caught in our own knowledge or views. Knowledge may be necessary to think and to discern, and may be helpful in many aspects of our daily life, but it is not the highest truth.

In Buddhism, we consider knowledge as an obstacle to true understanding, and views as a barrier to insight. Clinging to views can prevent us from arriving at a deeper, more profound understanding of reality.

We have to learn how to release the knowledge we currently possess. If someone climbing a ladder gets to the fourth rung and thinks they have reached the top, then they will not go any further. That is the end of their inquiry. We must know that there is a fifth rung in order to be able to reach it, and for this we need to let go of the fourth. We should not be caught in what we think we know. We have to be ready to release what we know in order to arrive at another level of knowing and understanding. In the Buddhist tradition, this is the most important thing—learning to release what we know.

The Buddha teaches us to look at things with the eyes of interbeing and to recognize their nature of dependent co-arising, that is, that all things arise in dependence on each other (*pratītya samutpāda*). When we are able to see in this way, we free ourselves from a world in which each thing appears to have an individual identity. The mind that sees things in their interbeing, dependent co-arising nature is called the mind of nondiscriminative wisdom. This is what we call Right View: the view that transcends all views. In Zen Buddhism there is an expression describing this insight: "The road of speech has been blocked, the path of the mind has been cut."

"Truth is found in life" and not merely in conceptual knowledge. We practice this by observing reality in ourselves and in the world at all times. Continually observing life means to practice mindfulness according to the method outlined in the Sutra on the Four Establishments of Mindfulness (Satipaṭṭhāna Sutta). This sutra teaches us how to be aware of what is going on in our body, in our feelings, in our mind, and in the objects of our mind, which is the world around us. The practice of mindfulness can help us develop concentration and insight, so that we can see reality as it is.

In the Sutra of One Hundred Parables, the Buddha tells the story of a young merchant and his son. The merchant, a widower, loved his son dearly, but lost him due to his lack of wisdom. One day, while the man was away, his little boy was kidnapped by a gang of bandits, who razed the entire village before fleeing. When the young merchant returned home, he found the charred remains of a child near where his house had been and, in his suffering and confusion, he mistook the charred remains for his own son. He cried unceasingly, arranged a cremation ceremony, and then carried the bag of ashes with him day and night tied around his neck. A few months later, his little boy was able to escape from the bandits and find his way home. At midnight, he knocked on the door of his father's rebuilt house, but the father, thinking that some mischievous boy was ridiculing him, refused to open the door. The boy knocked and knocked, but the merchant clung to his view that his boy was dead, and eventually his son had to go away. This father who could not let go of his wrong perception lost his son forever.

The Buddha said that when we are attached to views, even if the truth comes knocking on our door, we will refuse to let it in.

This training points out that wisdom, or insight, is collective. In an age of individualism such as ours, we are easily led to believe that our own view is right and we forget to listen to the views of others. By listening to others we come closer to the truth.

The Third Mindfulness Training
Freedom of Thought

Aware of the suffering brought about when we impose our views on others, we are determined not to force others, even our children, by any means whatsoever—such as authority, threat, money, propaganda, or indoctrination—to adopt our views. We are committed to respecting the right of others to be different, to choose what to believe and how to decide. We will, however, learn to help others let go of and transform fanaticism and narrowness through loving speech and compassionate dialogue.

This Third Mindfulness Training deals with the issue of freedom of thought. Respecting other peoples' viewpoints is a distinctive feature of Buddhism. The Kalama Sutta is one of the earliest charters for free inquiry. In it, the Buddha responds to a question concerning the problem of who or what to believe in and which doctrine is the best. The Buddha says, "It is fine to have doubt. Do not believe in something just because people think highly of it, or because it has come from tradition, or because it is found in scriptures. Consider whether it goes against your judgment, whether it could cause harm, whether it is condemned by wise people, and, above all, whether by putting it into practice it will bring about harm, destruction, or pain. Anything that you deem beautiful, that accords with your judgment, is appreciated by wise people, and once put into practice will bring about joy and happiness, can be accepted and put into practice."

Just as a shadow follows an object, the Third Mindfulness Training follows the Second, because an attitude of openness and nonattachment to views creates the necessary respect for the freedom of others. To be able to respect others' freedom, we need to free ourselves from attachment and fanaticism and help others to do the same. How can we help other people? Through "compassionate dialogue," which means having the capacity to use loving speech and to listen to others deeply, with an open mind, free of judgement. Compassionate dialogue is the essence of nonviolent action, *ahiṃsā*. Ahimsa begins with the energy of tolerance and loving kindness, which is expressed in gentle, compassionate, and skillful speech that can move people's hearts. This creates the conditions necessary for people to change. Understanding and compassion must be the basis of all nonviolent action. Actions motivated by anger or hatred cannot be described as nonviolent nor can they be described as wise.

As parents, we can respect freedom of thought in our

children, even if they are very young. We can learn a lot from our children. Each human being is unique in his or her characteristics, capacities, and preferences. We remain open in order to understand our children and refrain from merely imposing our views and beliefs on them. Although from the same tree, blossoms are not the same as the roots, leaves, and twigs. We should allow blossoms to be blossoms, leaves to be leaves, and twigs to be twigs, so that each can realize its highest capacity for development. As adults we can share our experience with our children and they in turn can express their feelings, intuitions, and ideas to us.

The Fourth Mindfulness Training
Awareness of Suffering

Aware that looking deeply at the nature of suffering can help us develop understanding and compassion, we are determined to come home to ourselves, to recognize, accept, embrace, and listen to our own suffering with the energy of mindfulness. We will do our best not to run away from our suffering or cover it up through consumption, but practice conscious breathing and walking to look deeply into the roots of our suffering. We know we can realize the path leading to the transformation of suffering only when we understand deeply the roots of suffering. Once we have understood our own suffering, we will be able to understand the suffering of others. We are committed to finding ways, including personal contact and using telephone, electronic, audiovisual, and other means, to be with those who suffer, so we can help them transform their suffering into compassion, peace, and joy.

The first Dharma talk given by the Buddha was on the Four Noble Truths. This First Truth is *duḥkha,* the presence of suffering. Recognizing the existence of suffering in our lives is the starting point of all Buddhist practice. If we are not aware that we are unwell, we do not know to seek treatment, and we cannot be healed. The Second Truth is that there are causes and conditions that lead to suffering. The Third is that happiness is possible; it is possible to transform suffering into joy and happiness. And the Fourth tells us how to do this; it outlines the path that leads to happiness. These are liberating truths.

This training is about being in touch (tiếp) with suffering. If we do not understand the origin of suffering, we shall not be able to see the path that leads out of suffering, both our own and that of others and the world. Only when we understand our own suffering can we truly understand the suffering of others and be able to help them. Earlier versions of the Fourteen Mindfulness Trainings did not highlight this important realization—that before we can help others we need to recognize the suffering in our own person and look deeply to see and understand its root causes. This is something many people have not yet managed to do. The problem today is that we run away from our own suffering. We are suffering but we do not have the courage to recognize it, to come back to ourselves and look deeply into the true nature of our suffering in order to take care of it. Instead we cover it up with consumption, using food, the phone, alcohol, music, drugs, magazines, novels, and the Internet. We use these things, not because we really need to use them, but because we do not want to be in touch with the suffering within us. We want to be in touch with the wonders of life and we want to help others, but we also need to be in touch with our own suffering. Only when we understand the roots of our suffering are we able to remove or transform it. When we can do this, we shall cease making others suffer. We have to understand ourselves first before we can understand someone else. If we don't do this, our own suffering will lead us into an abyss.

Suffering is not all bad. It can have a therapeutic power. It can help us open our eyes. Once we start facing the suffering within us we shall want to search for its cause, which means finding out what we have been feeding ourselves, what kinds of nutriments we are consuming that have brought about our suffering. We also want to find out the causes of the suffering in our society, but with this we need to be careful and exercise moderation. Being overwhelmed by too much suffering can destroy our capacity to love or to take appropriate action. We have to know our limits and find a healthy balance between being in touch with what is terrible in life and what is wonderful. We need to know how to water the good, positive seeds within us so we can bear the more distressing things. If the First Noble Truth explains the presence of suffering in life, the Third Truth recognizes that well-being is possible and encourages us to touch life's peace, joy, and happiness. When people say that Buddhism is pessimistic, it is because they are focusing on the First Noble Truth and overlooking the Third. Mahayana Buddhism takes great care to emphasize the Third Noble Truth. Its literature is full of references to the beautiful green willow, the violet bamboo, and the full moon as manifestations of the true Dharma. "The path leading to the transformation of suffering," which is mentioned in the text of the Fourth Mindfulness Trainings is the Noble Eightfold Path, the Fourth Noble Truth.[7] Whenever we practice any one of the eight elements of this path, it already brings us happiness.

Our suffering is interconnected with the suffering of other beings. When we are happy and at peace, we will not create suffering in others. When we work to alleviate the suffering in the world, we ourselves are the first to benefit. Practice is not just for our own sake, but we practice too for the good of others and society as a whole.

We pay attention to the problems of the world like hunger, disease, war, oppression, and social injustice, but we also practice stopping and coming back to ourselves by means of mindful breathing, sitting, walking, and studying the sutras, in order to be aware of both what is going on within ourselves

---

[7] The elements of the Noble Eightfold Path are: Right View, Right Thinking, Right Speech, Right Action, Right Livelihood, Right Diligence, Right Mindfulness, and Right Concentration.

and what is happening in the world. What is going on in the world is also going on within ourselves, and vice versa. Once we see this clearly, we cannot fail to take a stance or to act. When a village is being bombed and children and adults are wounded and dying, we cannot sit still in our temple or meditation hall. If we have compassion and wisdom, we will find ways to practice meditation while helping other people. There is a relationship between our own self nature and the nature of suffering, injustice, and war. To see into the true nature of the world's wars and weapons is to see into our own true nature.

Staying in touch with the reality of suffering nourishes the wellsprings of understanding (*prajñā*) and compassion (*karuṇā*) in us. It nourishes our Bodhisattva Vow to help all beings find a way out of suffering. If we cut ourselves off from the reality of suffering, whether our own or that of others, we cannot have compassion.

As parents we can find skillful ways to help our children stay in touch with the reality of suffering, without overwhelming them with a situation they feel they can do nothing about. For example, they can learn about how other children suffer from hunger and deprivation or how animals are mistreated, and we can help them find appropriate ways to respond to this. When we help children see and understand the suffering of humans and other living beings, we nourish compassion and understanding in them. We must practice in each moment of our daily life and not just in the meditation hall.

The Fifth Mindfulness Training
Compassionate, Healthy Living

Aware that true happiness is rooted in peace, solidity, freedom, and compassion, we are determined not to accumulate wealth while millions are hungry and dying nor to take as the aim of our life fame, power, wealth, or sensual pleasure, which can bring much suffering and despair. We will practice looking deeply into how we nourish our body and mind with edible foods, sense impressions, volition, and consciousness. We are committed not to gamble or to use alcohol, drugs or any other products which bring toxins into our own and the collective body and consciousness, such as certain websites, electronic games, music, TV programs, films, magazines, books, and conversations. We will consume in a way that preserves compassion, well-being, and joy in our body and consciousness and in the collective body and consciousness of our families, our society, and the Earth.

Like a branch growing out from the trunk of a tree, the Fifth Mindfulness Training emerges naturally from the Fourth. According to the Fourth Training, we learn to be in touch with suffering in order to transform it. In the Fifth we learn the best way to be happy. Our happiness comes from insight, understanding, and love, and not from fame, power, or wealth. Many people who are very rich, famous, or powerful continue to suffer greatly, and many even commit suicide. In our pursuit of wealth, power, or fame we do not have the time to enjoy the wonders of life and to realize the insight that can remove our suffering.

The Fifth Training also speaks about consumption and health. We have to consume in such a way as to keep our body and mind healthy. We have brought into this training the teaching on the Four Kinds of Nutriments we consume, namely edible foods, sense impressions, volition, and consciousness.

In our present-day society, people run after the enjoyment of material things. Many of us are not mindful or selective when it comes to what we consume, and we ingest items that are toxic for body and mind. Many of us are consuming edible foods that lead to disease.

As far as sense impressions are concerned, people search for a heightened feeling of pleasure that is brought on by the use of alcohol and drugs. In our time, even very young ones waste a great deal of time on electronic devices or the Internet. Children and parents do not have time to spend together or to be in touch with nature. What is more, all manner of toxic content is to be found on the Internet, and if we are not careful we can easily become addicted to it. That is why in this Training we mention the Internet as a real problem of our time.

In Plum Village when a monk or a nun wants to go on the Internet they have to have a second body. I do not know if this principle can be applied at home in the family. If our small child goes on the Internet alone, it can be very dangerous. They can lose their innocence and comsume or do things that harm their body and mind. The Internet is a sense-impression food we have to be very careful with.

The third kind of food is volition, what we want or desire. We need to have wishes for wholesome things: like protecting the environment, helping the poor and hungry, striving for social justice, educating for peace. The wish to find happiness in consumption is a toxic wish that will bring suffering and can even ruin our life. The desire to vent our anger, get revenge, or do something violent is also toxic volition.

The fourth source of food is consciousness: we consume our own thoughts. For example, if we suffered as a child; the suffering may still be there, and we may have the tendency to go back and ruminate on the suffering of the past. Continuing to consume like this is not good for our health. Instead, every time these things come up, we can recognize them, embrace them, and let them go. We go back to the present moment where there is light, sunshine, and blue sky, and where all the wonders of life are available. Practicing like this, we can transform the sufferings that lie deep in our consciousness. Once we have done it for ourselves, we can help another person to do it.

The Fifth Training is related to the matter of finding happiness. The reason why people consume unwholesome nutriments is that they are trying to be happy. But this kind of happiness has no substance. We try to avoid the difficulties and suffering that we do not know how to resolve, and we go in search of happiness in order to cover up that suffering. We drink alcohol. We open the refrigerator and take out something to eat in order to forget about our anxiety, our boredom, our loneliness, our sadness, and our feeling of being ill at ease. This is a sickness of our present-day society.

We need to live simply in order to remain as free as possible from the modern diseases that arise from stress. We resolve not to live the kind of life that is filled with pressure and anxiety. The only way out is to consume less and be content with fewer possessions. In Dharma sharing sessions, with others who share our concerns, we can find better ways to live simply and happily together. Once we are able to live simply and happily, we have more time and energy to share.

The Sixth Mindfulness Training
Taking Care of Anger

Aware that anger blocks communication and creates suffering, we are committed to taking care of the energy of anger when it arises, and to recognizing and transforming the seeds of anger that lie deep in our consciousness. When anger manifests, we are determined not to do or say anything, but to practice mindful breathing or mindful walking to acknowledge, embrace, and look deeply into our anger. We know that the roots of anger are not outside of ourselves but can be found in our wrong perceptions and lack of understanding of the suffering in ourselves and others. By contemplating impermanence, we will be able to look with the eyes of compassion at ourselves and at those we think are the cause of our anger, and to recognize the preciousness of our relationships. We will practice Right Diligence in order to nourish our capacity of understanding, love, joy, and inclusiveness, gradually transforming our anger, violence, and fear, and helping others do the same.

The Sixth Mindfulness Training advises us not to do or say anything when we are angry. The first thing to do when we get angry is to return to our breathing and practice mindfulness of breathing—following our breathing and allowing it time to calm down. Practicing mindful walking is also very helpful. We acknowledge that we're angry, and then we start to look deeply into the roots of our anger. Often the roots of our anger are found in ourselves. We may have wrong perceptions. Somebody may have said something that hurt us and we believe they did this on purpose. But they might just have been unskillful and had no idea that what they were saying would hurt us. They may have said the same kind of thing to somebody else and nothing happened, so how could they know this would hurt us?

We also need to understand that what they said or did may have come from their own suffering. We know from our own experience that when we are suffering, it is not always easy to practice loving speech. Maybe they upset us. We suffer and when we speak to them, there is no loving kindness in our voice. The practice of not doing or saying anything, especially when we're angry, can be quite challenging. How do we do this? When we live in a community and we get angry with somebody, don't we still have to keep speaking to that person? How can we keep on interacting calmly and civilly but not address the issue that made us angry? "Not to say anything," means not speaking with anger, but also not avoiding or blocking the other person out. It's a real practice, to keep on communicating mindfully, in a civil way, but not to address the issue until we have calmed down and looked into ourselves and seen what actually happened for us.

In 1975, after the end of the war in Vietnam, many Vietnamese people boarded boats, which were often overloaded or unseaworthy, to cross the Gulf of Thailand and reach Malaysia or Singapore. Many boats were attacked by pirates who robbed and raped the refugees. When I heard of the rape and suicide of a twelve-year-old girl and the drowning of her father, my first response was anger. But when I looked deeply, I realized that if I had been born and raised in the same social conditions along the coast of Thailand as these pirates, I would be a pirate now. A variety of interdependent causes has created the pirate. The responsibility for turning into a pirate does not lie solely with the pirate himself nor with his family, but with society as a whole. Each day hundreds of babies are being born into conditions of abject poverty near the Gulf of

Siam. If governments, politicians, educators, economists, and others do not do something to prevent it, twenty-five years from now many of these babies will have become criminals or pirates. Each of us shares some responsibility for the existence of pirates.

We all have the totality of all possible seeds in our store consciousness. Everyone has the potential to be angry, to hate, to be violent, even if those things have not manifested. When we speak about the "seeds of anger that lie deep in our consciousness" we are referring to the potential for anger, hate, and violence that lies within all of us, even if we are not angry or violent at the moment. This mindfulness training advises us to use preventative medicine so that these unwholesome seeds do not sprout. We might think it is impossible to transform unconscious anger and hatred, or that the best time to transform them is when we are already feeling angry. But in fact we can transform anger and hatred even before they arise. During sitting meditation, we can shine the light of awareness on our unpleasant feelings and thus identify their roots. We can look directly at feelings we usually prefer to avoid, and just by our looking at them they will already begin to transform. Then, when they rise up from our unconscious mind in the form of anger, they will not take us by surprise. We can plant seeds of love, compassion, and understanding in our daily lives, and those seeds will weaken the seeds of anger in us. We do not have to wait for the anger to arise to do this work. In fact, it will be much more difficult to do once anger has already arisen.

It may happen that we feel quite joyful and peaceful for a few weeks, but this does not mean that there were no seeds of anger lying dormant in our store consciousness or that they had not been watered during that time. For example, if someone says something that hurts us, we may not react right away. But several weeks later, we might become angry at that person for some very small reason. I like to tell the story of a young child who smeared excrement all over the walls of her living room. Her mother arduously tried to remove the mess and did not appear to be angry at all. But then, a few days later, the little girl accidentally spilled some soy sauce on the table and her mother just exploded. Obviously the seeds of anger had been watered when the child smeared the excrement on the walls, but her mother had suppressed her anger. This time though, for such a small accident, she had become extremely angry. So, if we are mindful, we can deal with our anger before it becomes a bomb ready to explode.

The Plum Village community practices the Peace Treaty, an agreement between family or community members for what to do when we get angry.[8]

When we are angry, what we generally forget to do is to come back to ourself and recognize that the main cause of our anger lies within us and is not the other person. When we are angry we need the time and space to withdraw from the situation. We practice mindful breathing and walking in order to recognize that we are suffering and to see that the cause of

[8] See Thich Nhat Hanh, *Touching Peace: Practicing the Art of Mindful Living*, Parallax, 1992.

our suffering lies in our hurt pride and our wrong perceptions. Once we are calm enough it will be easy to practice looking deeply in order to see the roots of our anger. Looking deeply into the other person helps us understand that they too suffer, and with that understanding and compassion arise.

How do we practice Right Diligence when dealing with strong emotions?

1. If the seeds of anger, violence, or fear have not arisen in our mind consciousness, we practice to transform them in the depths of our consciousness and we do our best not to put ourselves in a situation where they could be triggered.
2. If these seeds have already arisen, we find ways to calm them down and transform them.
3. If the beneficial seeds of understanding, love, joy, and inclusiveness have not arisen, we find ways to help them arise.
4. If they have arisen, we find ways to keep them in our mind consciousness for as long as possible.

There is also the practice of looking deeply into the impermanent nature of all things, which is an important element in transforming our anger. We recognize that the person with whom we are angry is impermanent and we do not know how much longer we shall be together. We do not want to waste the precious time we have by being angry with each other or ruin our relationship with our anger.

The Seventh Mindfulness Training
Dwelling Happily in the Present Moment

Aware that life is available only in the present moment, we are committed to training ourselves to live deeply each moment of daily life. We will try not to lose ourselves in dispersion or be carried away by regrets about the past, worries about the future, or craving, anger, or jealousy in the present. We will practice mindful breathing to be aware of what is happening in the here and the now. We are determined to learn the art of mindful living by touching the wondrous, refreshing, and healing elements that are inside and around us, in all situations. In this way, we will be able to cultivate seeds of joy, peace, love, and understanding in ourselves, thus facilitating the work of transformation and healing in our consciousness. We are aware that real happiness depends primarily on our mental attitude and not on external conditions, and that we can live happily in the present moment simply by remembering that we already have more than enough conditions to be happy.

The Buddha offered us the practice of mindfulness to help us come back to what is happening in the present moment, to be fully present and not dispersed in our thinking or carried away by regrets about the past, worries about the future, or craving, anger, and jealousy in the present. Mindfulness allows us to touch the wondrous, refreshing, and healing elements that are inside and around us, and to nourish the seeds of joy, peace, love, and understanding in ourselves.

Like the kernel of a peach, this mindfulness training is at the heart of the life of the Order of Interbeing. Whether you live at a meditation center, work in an office, live with your family, or study at a university, the practice of mindfulness, establishing ourselves fully in the present moment, is crucial. The Chinese character for mindfulness, 念, has two components: heart or mind, 心, and present moment, 今.

To be mindful means to bring the mind back to the present moment, to be fully present in the moment—not one part of you washing the dishes while another part is wondering when the work will be finished. We practice mindfulness the whole day long, while walking, sitting, standing, lying down, working, and resting; these are all occasions for practice. Conscious breathing is the vehicle that brings us back to the present moment, and keeps us there. The Sutra on the Full Awareness of Breathing and the Sutra on the Four Establishments of Mindfulness teach us how to be aware of what is going on in our body, our feelings, our mind, and to be aware of the objects of our mind, the world we perceive around us.[9]

[9] For sutra texts and commentaries, see: Thich Nhat Hanh, *Breathe, You Are Alive! The Sutra on the Full Awareness of Breathing*, Parallax, 1996, 2008; and Thich Nhat Hanh, *Transformation and Healing: Sutra on the Four Foundations of Mindfulness*, Parallax, 1990, 2006.

Sustained mindfulness leads to concentration and wisdom. We develop concentration and wisdom along with a deep sense of joy and happiness, because as we see more deeply into the true nature of reality, we see how wonderful are the world and all the different beings—animal, plant, and mineral—that inhabit it. Mindfulness enables us to be in touch with the wonderful flowers, the glorious moon, our children, our partner, our friends. These are all infinitely precious and rare, part of the interbeing nature of all things. Mindfulness makes life real, deep, and worth living. It helps us be in the here and now, where true life can be encountered. It helps us get in touch with the refreshing and healing elements within and around us. While practicing mindfulness, we plant and water the seeds of joy, peace, and understanding in us, seeds that have the power to alleviate and transform the pain and afflictions we carry. It is not necessary to touch these afflictions directly for healing to take place. Often our afflictions and pain transform on their own due to the presence of the positive seeds we plant and water in our daily life by the practice of mindful living.

The spirit of this training can be traced back to the Pali canon where we encounter the expression *dittha dhamma sukha vihāri*, which means to dwell happily in the present moment, in this very lifetime. We do not seek happiness in a distant future or in heaven after we die, but we cultivate happiness right in the present moment. Happiness is primarily a mental attitude, but we tend to think that our happiness depends on external conditions. As practitioners we use our mind to produce happiness. There are always conditions for happiness within us and around us; we only have to remind ourselves of them and we can be happy straightaway. Remembering past suffering can help us realize how much good fortune we have now and treasure the things we take for granted—legs to walk, eyes to see, the warmth of the sun, the sound of the rain. When we practice mindfulness and concentration, we create moments of happiness, and when we are nourished by happiness, we nourish those around us. Then when suffering arises, we will have the capacity to recognize, embrace, transform, and heal it.

If we are not happy and joyful in our practice, we shall not want to practice very long. Joy and happiness nourish our practice and make it stronger. If our practice does not transform our life and bring us great joy, if we are not able to bring joy to others and to understand them, we need to ask oursleves if we are practicing correctly. The wonders of the universe are revealed to us in the meditation on interdependence. We can see that for one thing to exist, everything else also needs to exist. "This is, because that is."

The Eighth Mindfulness Training
True Community and Communication

Aware that lack of communication always brings separation and suffering, we are committed to training ourselves in the practice of compassionate listening and loving speech. Knowing that true community is rooted in inclusiveness and in the concrete practice of the harmony of views, thinking, and speech, we will practice to share our understanding and experiences with members in our community in order to arrive at collective insight.

We are determined to learn to listen deeply without judging or reacting, and refrain from uttering words that can create discord or cause the community to break. Whenever difficulties arise, we will remain in our Sangha and practice looking deeply into ourselves and others to recognize all the causes and conditions, including our own habit energies, that have brought about the difficulties. We will take responsibility for all the ways we may have contributed to the conflict and keep communication open. We will not behave as a victim but be active in finding ways to reconcile and resolve all conflicts, however small.

The essence of the Eighth Training is compassionate communication, which is the foundation for living together in harmony in our relationships, within the family, or in community. The training mentions three of the Six Harmonies, 六 和, taught by the Buddha as necessary pillars for community life—the Harmonies of Speech, Thinking, and Views.[10] The Harmony of Speech is born from understanding, patience, and refraining from blaming; practicing kind speech, we

[10] The other three harmonies are: living together in one place; sharing the same resources; and observing the same mindfulness trainings. The Six Harmonies have been practiced by Buddhist communities since the time of the Buddha and are still relevant.

avoid quarrels. The Harmony of Thinking is based on practicing together and sharing an understanding of the Dharma. It is what leads us to understand the other. The way we think about each other is very important. A loving thought gives rise to loving speech and actions, which in turn will bring us health and happiness, and bring happiness to the world. The Harmony of Views is what helps us to arrive at a collective insight. This is a deep practice of not being caught in our own point of view. When we go to a meeting or have a discussion of any kind, we may have a point of view that we consider to be correct. We have the right, and sometimes the duty, to express our point of view. But it is also our duty to listen to all other points of view with an open mind and let go of our own point of view as soon as we see there is a better way of seeing the situation.

There may be times when difficulties arise in our family, our community, or at work. The Training tells us that at these times we must put all our heart into finding ways to reconcile, beginning by being aware that we ourselves have contributed to the difficulty. It may be necessary to invite a senior Order member to help us practice Beginning Anew to resolve the conflict.[11] Behaving as a victim, blaming, attributing what has gone wrong to the unskillfulness of others, and believing there is nothing we ourselves can say or do about it, is playing a passive role. We need to actively assume responsibility for

[11] Beginning Anew is the practice of reconciliation in the Plum Village tradition. See Sister Chan Khong, *Beginning Anew: Four Steps to Restoring Communication*, Parallax, 2014.

our part in the difficulty or conflict that has arisen and work together to find a solution.

Mediation is an art, requiring us to understand both sides of a conflict. Not only do both sides bear partial responsibility, but even those who are not directly involved in the conflict bear some responsibility. If we had lived in mindfulness, we could have seen the earliest phases of the conflict beginning to arise, and we could have helped avoid it. To reconcile is not to judge by standing outside of a conflict. It is to take some responsibility for the existence of the conflict and to make every effort to understand the suffering of both sides. Then we can communicate to each side the suffering experienced by the other side, and offer some resolution based on an ideal common to both sides.

When we ourselves are part of the conflict, our awareness of the need for reconciliation and of our duty to work for it will empower us to act, and the success of our efforts will depend on the degree of our understanding and compassion. The purpose of reconciliation is not to save face or serve self-interest, but to realize understanding and compassion. To help reconcile, we ourselves must embody understanding and compassion.

The Ninth Mindfulness Training
Truthful and Loving Speech

Aware that words can create happiness or suffering, we are committed to learning to speak truthfully, lovingly, and constructively.

We will use only words that inspire joy, confidence, and hope as well as promote reconciliation and peace in ourselves and among other people. We will speak and listen in a way that can help ourselves and others to transform suffering and see the way out of difficult situations. We are determined not to say untruthful things for the sake of personal interest or to impress people, nor to utter words that might cause division or hatred. We will protect the happiness and harmony of our Sangha by refraining from speaking about the faults of other persons in their absence and always ask ourselves whether our perceptions are correct. We will speak only with the intention to understand and help transform the situation. We will not spread rumors nor criticize or condemn things of which we are not sure. We will do our best to speak out about situations of injustice, even when doing so may make difficulties for us or threaten our safety.

There are four kinds of Right Speech according to the Sutra on the Ten Good Actions (Taisho 600): speaking the truth, not embellishing or exaggerating the truth, not speaking divisively, and not using insulting or abusive language.[12] This also includes gossip, which in the words of the mindfulness training is "not spreading rumors" and "refraining from speaking about the faults of other persons in their absence."

Of course it is important to train ourselves to always speak

[12] See Sūtra of the Path of the Ten Good Karmas at: 十善業道經 digital Chinese Canon T15n0600.

the truth, but we also have to know *how* to speak the truth. If we say something that deeply hurts or offends another person, we cannot excuse this by saying: "Well, I was only telling the truth." We need to be compassionate and choose skillful means to say something.

Because we want to impress people or make sure that they agree with us, we sometimes exaggerate the truth, for example, we may make someone's small mistake seem like a very serious mistake.

To speak divisively is to speak in a way that brings about division or discord between people. Maybe we do not like someone and we want others to dislike them too so we speak in such a way that brings about division between this person and the people who formerly liked them.

We know what it is to insult someone to their face but we can also insult someone when they are not present. This training reminds us not to talk badly about people in their absence; a phenomenon that is often found in the workplace. When we are with others who are gossiping, we can politely remind them to stop or excuse ourselves from the conversation.

Right speech always goes hand in hand with deep listening. When we listen deeply, we listen with the sole purpose of understanding the other person. When we understand them, their suffering and difficulties, we feel with them and compassionate speech comes easily.

When we speak, we can either create a world of love, trust, and happiness, or we can create a hell. We should be very careful about what we say and how we say it. If we are in the habit of talking too much, we can practice talking less. We must become more aware of our words and their effect on others. During retreats, we have the opportunity to practice silence, reducing our speaking by at least ninety percent, which can be extremely beneficial. Not only do we learn to recognize our habit energies around speaking—always speaking, speaking too much, too loudly, too quickly, not wanting to speak, and so on—but we can also learn to recognize if our speech is wholesome or not. Silence helps us reflect and see ourselves, the people around us, and life more clearly. When we have the opportunity to be in silence, space opens up for us to look deeply and smile at the flowers, the grass, the bushes, the trees, the birds, and our fellow human beings. If you have ever observed periods of complete silence, you will know the benefits of such practice. With silence, a smile, and right speech, we develop peace within ourselves and the world around us. Right speech builds understanding and reconciliation. The Ninth Mindfulness Training not only requires us to be honest with ourselves, but to have courage as well. How many of us are brave enough to speak out about situations of injustice, even when doing so might threaten our own safety?

The Tenth Mindfulness Training
Protecting and Nourishing the Sangha

Aware that the essence and aim of a Sangha is the practice of understanding and compassion, we are determined not to use the Buddhist community for personal power or profit, or transform our community into a political instrument. As members of a spiritual community, we should nonetheless take a clear stand against oppression and injustice. We should strive to change the situation, without taking sides in a conflict. We are committed to learning to look with the eyes of interbeing and to seeing ourselves and others as cells in one Sangha body. As a true cell in the Sangha body, generating mindfulness, concentration, and insight to nourish ourselves and the whole community, each of us is at the same time a cell in the Buddha body. We will actively build brotherhood and sisterhood, flow as a river, and practice to develop the three real powers—understanding, love, and cutting through afflictions—to realize collective awakening.

Building Sangha is our most noble task, and our first step in building Sangha is to become part of a Sangha whether it has already been founded or whether we found it ourselves. We all need a Sangha to support our personal practice and transformation. A Sangha flows like a river so that we do not evaporate as an individual drop of water. The world needs spiritual communities because they contribute a collective energy of peace to the world.

As a member of a Sangha we take care to strengthen our basic practice of mindful breathing, walking, and eating. Our own stable presence and practice of mindfulness is our best contribution to the Sangha. Just as in an animal or plant body the different cells of the body act their best for the body to be healthy, we are always aware of the fact that we are only a cell in the body. The human body is an organism with trillions of cells working together in harmony, with no boss.

In the context of a Sangha we have a very good opportunity to realize no-self. We understand that no individual becomes enlightened; enlightenment is collective. The Sangha is the environment in which we develop brotherhood and sisterhood and can care for each other as brothers and sisters of the same family.[13]

At times of division in our nation the Sangha has to be careful not to take sides, thus becoming partisan and exclusive. We want to protect our Sangha from becoming a political instrument because the true purpose of a religious community is to guide people on the spiritual path. Regrettably, in order to secure their government's support, religious communities often refrain from speaking out against oppression and injustices committed by their government. A spiritual community, however, should "take a clear stand against oppression and

[13] For more on Sangha building, see Thich Nhat Hanh, *Friends on the Path*, Parallax, 2002.

injustice." This should be done with a clear voice, based on the principles of the Four Noble Truths. The truth concerning the unjust situation should be fully exposed (the First Truth: the suffering). The various causes of injustice should be enumerated (the Second Truth: the causes and conditions that have led to this suffering). The purpose and desire for removing the injustice should be made obvious (the Third Truth: the removal of suffering). The measures for removing the injustice should be proposed (the Fourth Truth: the way to end suffering). Although the Sangha does not take sides, it can use its influence to change society. Speaking out is the first step, proposing and supporting appropriate measures for change is the next. Most important is to transcend all partisan conflicts. The voice of caring and understanding must be distinct from the voice of ambition. In any kind of conflict we need to develop compassion by understanding the difficulties and suffering of both sides.

The Eleventh Mindfulness Training
Right Livelihood

Aware that great violence and injustice have been done to our environment and society, we are committed not to live with a vocation that is harmful to humans and nature. We will do our best to select a livelihood that contributes to the well-being of all species on Earth and helps realize our ideal of understanding and compassion. Aware of economic, political, and social realities around the world, as well as our interrelationship with the ecosystem, we are determined to behave responsibly as consumers and as citizens. We will not invest in or purchase from companies that contribute to the depletion of natural resources, harm the Earth, or deprive others of their chance to live.

Right Livelihood is one of the elements of the Noble Eightfold Path. It urges us to practice a profession that harms neither humans nor nature, physically or morally. We live in a society where jobs are hard to find and it is difficult to practice Right Livelihood. Still, if our work happens to entail harming life, we should try our best to find another job. Our vocation can nourish our understanding and compassion, or it can erode them.

Many modern industries, including food manufacturing and agriculture, are harmful to humans and the planet. Most current farming practices are far from Right Livelihood. The chemical toxins used in modern farming methods harm the environment. Practicing Right Livelihood has become a difficult task for farmers. If they do not use chemical pesticides, it may be hard to compete commercially. Not many farmers have the courage to practice organic farming. Right Livelihood has ceased to be a purely personal matter. It is our collective karma.

If I were a schoolteacher and believed that nurturing love and understanding in children was the most beautiful occupation and a good example of Right Livelihood, I would probably object if someone were to ask me to stop teaching and become, for example, a butcher. However, if I meditate on the interrelatedness of all things, I see that the butcher is not solely responsible for the killing of animals. He kills them for all of us who want to eat meat and who buy pieces of raw meat, cleanly wrapped and displayed at our local supermarket. The act of killing is a collective one. In forgetfulness, we may separate ourselves from the butcher, thinking his livelihood is wrong, while ours is right. However, if we didn't eat meat, the abattoirs wouldn't kill or would kill less. This is why Right Livelihood is a collective matter. The choices and livelihood of each person affect all of us.

Millions of people make a living from the arms industry, manufacturing "conventional" and nuclear weapons. These so-called conventional weapons are sold to developing countries. People in these countries need food, not guns, tanks, or bombs. The United States, Russia, France, Germany, and China, are the top five suppliers of these weapons.[14] Manufacturing and selling weapons is certainly not Right Livelihood, but the responsibility for this situation does not lie solely with those who work in the arms industry. All of us—politicians, industrialists, manufacturers, corporations, economists, and consumers—share the responsibility for

[14] Pieter D. Wezeman et al., "Trends in International Arms Transfers, 2018," Stockholm International Peace Research Institute, March 2019. https://www.sipri.org/publications/2019/sipri-fact-sheets/trends-international-arms-transfers-2018.

the death and destruction caused by these weapons. We do not see clearly enough, we do not speak out, and we do not organize enough national debates on this huge problem. If we could discuss these issues globally, solutions could be found. New jobs must be created so that we do not have to live off the profits of weapons manufacturing.

If we are able to work in a profession that helps us realize our ideal of compassion, we can be very grateful. Every day, we can help create proper jobs for ourselves and others by living simply and healthily. Awakening and helping others to awaken is the very essence of Buddhist practice.

A newspaper reporter once asked me how we could prevent corporations from destroying the environment for the sake of making a profit. I said that giving them a Dharma talk about the harm they are doing would not address the root cause. The root of the problem is that making a profit is many people's idea of happiness. We need to allow them to taste other kinds of happiness that don't harm the environment, which is why we organize retreats for businesspeople, so that they can experience for themselves another kind of happiness, a deep and real happiness, which does not harm themselves, others, or our precious planet.

The Twelfth Mindfulness Training
Reverence for Life

Aware that much suffering is caused by war and conflict, we are determined to cultivate nonviolence, compassion, and the insight of interbeing in our daily lives and promote peace education, mindful mediation, and reconciliation within families, communities, ethnic and religious groups, nations, and in the world. We are committed not to kill and not to let others kill. We will not support any act of killing in the world, in our thinking, or in our way of life. We will diligently practice deep looking with our Sangha to discover better ways to protect life, prevent war, and build peace.

In every country in the world, killing human beings is condemned. But the Buddhist training to practice non-killing extends even further, to include all living beings. However, no one, not even a Buddha or a bodhisattva, can practice this mindfulness training to perfection. When we take a small step or boil a cup of water, we kill many tiny living beings. The essence of this training is to make every effort to respect and protect life, to continuously move in the direction of peace and reconciliation. We can try our best, even if we cannot succeed one hundred percent.

This mindfulness training is closely linked with the Eleventh. The way we live and how and what we consume affects the lives and security of humans and other living beings. There are many types of violence. War is a clear example. It is often caused by fanaticism and narrowness or by the will to gain political influence or economic power. The exploitation of one society by another that is technologically or politically stronger is another form of violence. We can oppose wars once they have started, but it is better to do our best to prevent them from breaking out. The way to prevent war is to make peace. We accomplish this first in our daily life by combating fanaticism and attachment to views—starting with ourselves—and working for social justice. We have to work vigorously against the political and economic ambitions of any country, including our own. If important issues like these are not debated on national and international levels, we will never be able to prevent societal violence.

We begin by studying and practicing this mindfulness training of non-killing in our daily lives. If we do not live our daily lives mindfully, we ourselves are responsible, to some extent, for the systemic violence in the world. Every year, around three million children die due to malnutrition.[15] The amount of grain used in Western countries to make liquor and feed cattle, for example, is enormous. Scientists have said that if we reduced meat and alcohol consumption in the West by fifty percent, the grains that would become available would be enough to solve all hunger and malnutrition problems in developing countries. Deaths and injuries caused by car accidents and cardiovascular and other modern Western illnesses would also be reduced in the West if the consumption of

[15] UNICEF, 2019: https://www.unicef.org/nutrition/.

liquor and meat decreased.

Defense budgets across the world continue to be mammoth, often at the expense of health and social welfare. Studies show that if we could stop or significantly slow down the manufacture of weapons, we would have more than enough money to erase poverty, hunger, ignorance, and many diseases from the world. In our busy daily lives, do we have enough time to look deeply into this mindfulness training of non-killing? How many among us can honestly say that we are doing enough to practice this training?

The Thirteenth Mindfulness Training
Generosity

Aware of the suffering caused by exploitation, social injustice, stealing, and oppression, we are committed to cultivating generosity in our way of thinking, speaking, and acting. We will practice loving kindness by working for the happiness of people, animals, plants, and minerals, and sharing our time, energy, and material resources with those who are in need. We are determined not to steal and not to possess anything that should belong to others. We will respect the property of others, but will try to prevent others from profiting from human suffering or the suffering of other beings.

Bringing to our awareness the pain caused by social injustice, the Thirteenth Mindfulness Training urges us to work for a more just, humane, and equitable society. This training is closely linked with the Fourth (Awareness of Suffering), the Fifth (Simple, Healthy Living), the Eleventh (Right Livelihood), and the Twelfth (Reverence for Life). In order to understand this Mindfulness Training deeply, we need to meditate on those four other trainings.

Exploitation, social injustice, stealing, and oppression come in many forms. We have to work on an individual level and as a community to examine our situation, exercising our intelligence and ability to look deeply so that we can discover appropriate ways to express loving kindness (*maitrī*, the love that brings joy to others) and address the real problems of our time.

Suppose we want to help those who are suffering under a brutal dictatorship. We know from experience that sending in troops to overthrow their government will destabilize the country and cause the death of many innocent people. By looking more deeply, with loving kindness, we may realize that the best time to help is before a country falls into the hands of a dictator. Offering young people of that country the opportunity to learn democratic ways of governing would be a good investment for peace in the future. If we wait until the situation gets bad, it may be too late. If we practice together with politicians, the military, business leaders, lawyers, legislators, artists, writers, and teachers, we can find the best ways for them to practice compassion, loving kindness, and understanding in their various settings and situations.

We need to practice being generous. Wanting to be generous and actually doing something about it are not the same. We may want to help others be happy, yet we are so caught up in the problems of our own daily lives. Sometimes just one pill or a little rice would be enough to save the life of a sick or hungry child, but we may think we do not have the time to help. It costs only about twenty cents to provide both lunch and dinner for a poor child in many countries. There are many simple things like this we can do to help people. We do not need to let our busy lifestyle prevent us from taking action.

Developing ways to prevent others from profiting from human suffering is the primary duty of legislators, politicians, and revolutionary leaders, those who want to make a better society. However, each of us can also contribute. We can stand in solidarity with the oppressed and help them protect their right to life and defend themselves against oppression and exploitation. The Bodhisattva Vows are immense, and each of us can be a true Bodhisattva and help deliver people from suffering.

The Fourteenth Mindfulness Training
True Love

For lay members: *Aware that sexual desire is not love and that sexual relations motivated by craving cannot dissipate the feeling of loneliness but will create more suffering, frustration, and isolation, we are determined not to engage in sexual relations without mutual understanding, love, and a deep long-term commitment. We resolve to find spiritual support for the integrity of our relationships from family members, friends, and sangha with whom there is support and trust. We know that to preserve the happiness of ourselves and others, we must respect the rights and commitments of ourselves and others. Recognizing the diversity of human experience, we are committed not to discriminate against any form of gender identity or sexual orientation. Seeing that body and mind are interrelated, we are committed to learning appropriate ways to take care of our sexual energy and cultivating loving kindness, compassion, joy, and inclusiveness for our own happiness and the happiness of others. We must be aware of future suffering that may be caused by sexual relations. We will treat our bodies with compassion and respect. We are determined to look deeply into the Four Nutriments and learn ways to preserve and channel our vital energies (sexual, breath, spirit) for the realization of our bodhisattva ideal. We will do everything in our power to protect children from sexual abuse and to prevent couples and families from being broken by sexual misconduct. We will be fully aware of the responsibility of bringing new lives into the world and will meditate regularly upon their future environment.*

For monastic members: *Aware that the deep aspiration of a monk or a nun can only be realized when he or she wholly leaves behind the bonds of sensual love, we are committed to practicing chastity and to helping others protect themselves. We are aware that loneliness and suffering cannot be alleviated through a sexual relationship, but through practicing loving kindness, compassion, joy, and inclusiveness. We know that a sexual relationship will destroy our monastic life, will prevent us from realizing our ideal of serving living beings, and will harm others. We will learn appropriate ways to take care of our sexual energy. We are determined not to suppress or mistreat our body, or look upon our body as only an instrument, but will learn to handle our body with compassion and respect. We will look deeply into the Four Nutriments in order to preserve and channel our vital energies (sexual, breath, spirit) for the realization of our bodhisattva ideal.*

In our present-day society there is much sexual desire but very little love. This creates a huge amount of suffering, not only for individuals, but also within families and in society. Every one of us needs to cultivate true love and take care of sexual desire. This precept is an attempt to make everyone aware of how important this is.

So many individuals, children, couples, and families have been wounded by sexual misconduct. Practicing this training is to prevent ourselves and others from being wounded. Our stability and the stability of our families and society depend on it. To practice the Fourteenth Mindfulness Training is to heal ourselves and our society.

In the past, Eastern and Western views about protecting our mind and body were probably quite similar: namely, just as we only share the deepest and most intimate things of our mind with someone we trust and love as a very close friend, the same is true of our body. If there is not a very deep bond of love between two people, they do not entrust their bodies to each other. This makes sexual love something very sacred. If you look on the body of another as just a tool to bring you sensual pleasure, your sexual relationship will lose its sacredness.

The body and mind are not two separate realities. Those who have been sexually abused feel that they have lost something very precious, and that feeling of loss and woundedness can last a whole lifetime. The wholeness of our body is related to the wholeness of our mind. The insight that the body and mind are two aspects of the same reality is very important. The body is to be found in the mind and the mind is to be found in the body. The union of two bodies can only be positive when there is also understanding and communion on the level of the spirit.

It is necessary to see that the body of your partner is a sacred place that needs all of your respect. As far as spiritual values are concerned, only when the other person has become your closest lifetime friend do you entrust your body and mind to them. Sexual communion should be accompanied by mindfulness, great respect, care, and love.

Even when two people are married or in a long-term committed relationship, they continue to show great respect toward each other, as they would toward an esteemed guest in the house. If every day you continue to discover what is deep and wonderful in the other person, then your love can continue for a whole lifetime.

How can we take care of the energy of sexual desire in our highly sexualized society? We need to guard our senses and practice mindful consumption. We receive so many sense impressions in our daily life—sounds and images from advertising, social media, the Internet, books, films, magazines—that water the seeds of sexual desire. Sex is used pervasively in our society as a means for selling products. To take care of sexual energy means not to allow the media or Internet to water seeds of sexual desire. Practicing mindfulness, we are able to distance ourselves from inappropriate films, books, and conversations.

The way, where, what, and how much we eat and drink can also influence the amount of sexual energy we have. It is helpful not to eat meat or drink alcohol as this affects our mind. It can reduce our impulse control and increase desire. We should always eat with moderation, especially in the evening. Regular exercise, qigong, yoga, and tai chi can also help moderate sexual energy, as well as meditation and finding an outlet for our creative expression.

The four basic elements of true love in Buddhism are loving kindness, compassion, joy, and equanimity. Practicing these elements will help increase our own happiness and that of the other person. Together we can increase these elements in our love daily. We need to organize regular sessions of Dharma sharing to be able to learn from each other how to practice this training well.

True love also means accepting the other person as they are, with all their strengths and weaknesses. The expression "long-term commitment" helps us understand the word "love." A long-term commitment between two people is only the beginning. For a tree to be strong, it needs to send many roots deep into the soil. If a tree has only one root, it may be blown over by the wind. The life of a couple also needs to be supported by many elements—family, friends, ideals, practice, and Sangha. This is why our relationship should be made known to our Sangha, friends, or family.

Responsibility is key in our practice. We need mindfulness in order to have a sense of responsibility toward others. In a community of practice, if there is no sexual misconduct, there will be stability and peace. You respect, support, and protect each other as Dharma brothers and sisters. We refrain from sexual misconduct because we are responsible for the well-being of so many people. If we are irresponsible, we can destroy everything. Practicing this training, we keep the Sangha beautiful.

Widespread loneliness, advertising, increasing sexualization in society all make it difficult to practice this training. The feeling of loneliness is universal. When there is no good communication between ourselves and other people, even in our own family, the feeling of loneliness and desire for love may cause us to search for intimacy in sexual relationships. But the belief that engaging in sexual relations will help us feel less lonely is a myth. In fact, if this is our motivation, we will feel even more lonely afterward. When there is not enough communication with another person on the level of the heart and spirit, a sexual relationship will only widen the gap and create more suffering for us both. If this is the basis of the relationship, it will be stormy, and we will make each other suffer.

In practicing the Fourteenth Mindfulness Training, we should always look into the nature of our love in order to see and not be fooled by our feelings. Sometimes we tell ourselves that we love the other person, but maybe that love is only an attempt to satisfy our egoistic needs. Maybe we have not looked deeply enough to see the needs of the other person. We must remember to look at one another as human beings with the capacity of becoming a Buddha, and not as an object of desire or as something to satisfy our needs. Unless we understand the other person's needs, aspirations, and difficulties, it is not true love.

In Asia, we say there are three sources of energy—sexual, breath, and spirit. Sexual energy is the type of energy that we expend during sexual intercourse. Vital breath is the energy we expend when we speak too much and breathe too little. Spirit is the energy we expend when we worry too much.

We need to know how to maintain a good balance of these energies, or we may act irresponsibly. According to Eastern medicine, if these three sources of energy are depleted, the body will weaken and disease will appear. Then it will be more difficult to practice.

After several years of ascetic practice, Śākyamuni Buddha realized that mistreating his body was a mistake, and he abandoned that practice. He saw that both indulging in sensual pleasure and mistreating his body were extremes to be avoided, that both lead to degeneration of mind and body. As a result, he adopted a Middle Way between the two extremes.

When practicing conscious breathing—counting the breath or following the breath—we do not waste the vital breath energy, instead we strengthen it. Concentration and the enjoyment of meditation do not expend spirit, but strengthen it. In Taoism and also in the martial arts, there are practices for preserving and nourishing these three sources of energy. You can learn ways to channel your sexual energy into deep realizations in the domains of art and meditation.

In the Buddha's time, a typical monk was a quiet person who practiced walking and sitting meditation both day and night. He carried a bowl into the local villages every morning to beg for food and would give a short Dharma talk to each layperson who donated some food. This way of life enabled him to preserve both vital breath and spirit energy.

In the time of the Buddha, the main reason for monks abstaining from sexual activity was to preserve energy. This is a point of commonality between Buddhism and most other Eastern spiritual and medical traditions. During the most difficult periods of his nonviolent struggles, Mahatma Gandhi also practiced abstinence, and he advised his colleagues to do the same as a way of coping with tense, difficult situations. Strength of spirit depends on these three sources of energy. In Vietnamese, the word "spiritual" (*tinh thần*) is formed by combining the words for sexual energy (*tinh*) and spirit (*thần*). The material and the spiritual are no longer distinct, and the name of each is used for the other. Those who have fasted know that if the three sources of energy are not preserved, you cannot fast for long. In 1966, the monk Thích Trí Quang was able to fast in Vietnam for one hundred days, to draw attention to the suffering of his people because of the war. He could only do this because he knew how to preserve his three sources of energy.

The second reason that monks in the Buddha's time refrained from sexual activity was that they wanted to concentrate on their career of enlightenment. If a monk had a family to support and take care of, he would have had little time left for practice. Today many monks and priests are continually busy, even though they do not have wives or children. Just having to take care of their temples and religious communities, they are as busy as householders. One day the monk Dai San complained to his friend that he was too busy, and his friend replied, "Why don't you become a monk?" A monk is not supposed to be so busy. If he has no time to practice, there is really no reason to remain a monk.

The third reason that monks in the Buddha's time refrained from sexuality was to cut off "the chain of rebirth" (*samsāra*). The first meaning of rebirth means to be reborn in our offspring, our children, and grandchildren. During the time of the Buddha, much more so than in our own time, poverty and disease were the common lot for most people. Imagine a family with too many children, all of them frail and ill. There is a permanent shortage of food, no medicine, and no means of contraception. Each year a new child is born. This is still common in many parts of our world, and both parents and children suffer enormously. Rebirth must be understood in this context and with this background. For these people, a new birth is often not a joy, but a catastrophe. To give birth to a child is to perpetuate the cycle of hunger and disease. This is the continuation of samsāra. Therefore the mindfulness training for celibacy during the time of the Buddha also aimed at preventing unwanted childbirths.

We can see how this mindfulness training is directly related to issues of population, hunger, and economic development. For more than twenty centuries, the presence of Buddhist monks in countries like Sri Lanka, Burma, Thailand, Laos, Cambodia, China, Vietnam, Korea, Tibet, and Mongolia, has contributed significantly to reducing the world's population. The population explosion is one of the most serious problems of our day. Hunger leads to war and, in our times, wars are incredibly destructive. Countries that cannot control their population cannot overcome poverty.

There is the threat of nuclear holocaust. There are the realities of climate change, habitat and environmental destruction, species extinction, rising oceans, mass migration and refugees, and the depletion of natural resources. We must be aware of the actual situation of the world. We should reflect on the future into which we are sending our children, to motivate us to act and live in a way that can create a better future for ourselves and our children.

The answer is not to stop having children, but to make the world a better place. The future of the Earth and the future of our children depend on the way we live today. If we continue to exploit and destroy our ecosystems, if we continue to allow our greed to destroy the Earth and all her wonders, if we do not curb the growth of the world's population, the Earth and humankind will not have a future. The way each of us lives is a building block for a future of peace. The Fourteenth Mindfulness Training is vast, and its observance is linked to all the other mindfulness trainings of the Order of Interbeing.

The Fourteen Mindfulness Trainings of the Order of Interbeing are the essence of the Buddha's teachings. They are not just ideas; they show us how to concretely apply mindfulness in our daily lives. If we practice these trainings deeply, we will recognize that each one contains all the others. Studying and practicing the Mindfulness Trainings can help us understand the true nature of interbeing—we cannot just be by ourselves alone; we can only inter-be with everyone and everything else. To practice these trainings is to become aware of what is going on in our bodies, our minds, and the world. With awareness, we can live our lives happily, fully present in each moment we are alive, intelligently seeking solutions to the problems we face, and working for peace in small and large ways.

When you practice the Five Mindfulness Trainings deeply, you are already practicing the Fourteen.[16] If you want

[16] Vide supra footnote 2, p. xxi.

to formally receive the Fourteen Mindfulness Trainings and enter the core community of the Order of Interbeing, it is because you wish to build Sangha and help organize the practice in a Sangha. If this is not the case, the Five Mindfulness Trainings are enough. You can practice the Fourteen without a formal ceremony, without being ordained as a member of the Order.

Many people of all religious faiths deeply appreciate the teachings of the Fourteen Mindfulness Trainings. A Jewish Rabbi was inspired to make a version of the ten commandments, beginning each of them with the words, "Aware of the suffering caused by. . . ."[17] Please feel free to modify a few words of the trainings, to make them relevant and applicable to your own tradition, whether Christian, Jewish, Islamic, or other teachings. I hope you will join me in practicing these Mindfulness Trainings or the equivalent in your own tradition. It is crucial for our own well-being and the well-being of our world that we practice a global ethic together.

---

[17] Rami Shapiro in *Minyan: Ten Principles for Living a Life of Integrity* (New York: Harmony Books, 1997).

Part Three

The Charter of the Order of Interbeing

Introduction to the Charter of the Order of Interbeing

Dear Reader, this is the 1996 revised version of the Charter, and it is ripe for revision again since it does not represent the present situation in the Order as far as some practicalities are concerned. As the Charter itself states, all past versions of the Charter should be preserved because they have an historical value as to the evolution of the Order. So we are presenting the Charter here as an historical document. The basic principles of practice mentioned in the Charter are still valid and an important part of the life of the Order.

According to the Charter of the Order of Interbeing, the aim of the Order is to make Buddhism relevant to our own time. It's members study, experience, and apply it in a versatile and effective way in their own life and that of society. They have the aspiration of a bodhisattva to help others.

The Charter lists four principles as the foundation of the Order: nonattachment from views; direct realization of the nature of interdependent origination through mindfulness and meditation; appropriateness; and Skillful Means.[18] Let us

[18] "Appropriateness" according to the Two Relevances means: 1) relevance to the Buddha's teachings (契理) and 2) relevance to the people being taught (契機).

examine each of these principles.

1. Nonattachment from views: To be attached means to be caught in dogmas, prejudices, habits, and what we consider to be the truth. The first aim of the practice is to be free of all attachments, especially attachment to views. This is the most important teaching of Buddhism.

2. Direct realization of the truth through meditation. This means the practice of concentration, or stopping and looking deeply, in order to realize the truth of interbeing. There are many guided meditations in the book *Blooming of a Lotus* or *Touching the Earth* which help us look deeply into interdependence.[19]

3. Relevance: A teaching, in order to bring about understanding and compassion, must reflect the needs of people and the realities of society. To do this, it must meet two criteria: it must conform to the basic tenets of Buddhism, and it must be truly helpful and relevant for the people who receive it. It is said that there are 84,000 Dharma doors through which one can enter Buddhism. For Buddhism to continue as a living source of wisdom and peace, even more doors should be opened.

---

[19] Thich Nhat Hanh, *Blooming of a Lotus: Guided Meditation Exercises for Healing and Transformation* (Boston: Beacon Press, 1993).
Thich Nhat Hanh, *Touching the Earth: Intimate Conversations with the Buddha* (Berkeley: Parallax, 2004).

4. Skillful Means (*upāya*): Skillful Means refers to the language, images, methods, and practices used by intelligent teachers to show the Buddha's Way and guide people in their efforts to practice the Way in their own particular circumstances. These means are called Dharma doors.

Concerning these four principles, the Charter expresses in Chapter II, item six, that the spirit of nonattachment from views and the spirit of direct realization of the truth are the two most important guides for attaining true understanding. They lead to objectivity, inclusiveness, and compassion in the way we perceive the world and relate to others. The principles of the Two Relevances and Skillful Means are guides for actions in society. They lead to creativity and the realization of nonduality, which are essential for the development and the accomplishment of our vow to help all beings. The teachings of nonattachment from views, direct realization of the truth, the Two Relevances, and Skillful Means can be found in all the most important sutras, such as the Prajñaparamitā sutras, the Lotus Sutra, the Avataṃsaka Sūtra and the Sutta Nipāta

Guided by these four principles, the Order of Interbeing has an open attitude toward all Buddhist schools. According to item four, the Order does not consider any sutra or group of sutras as its basic scripture(s). Inspiration is drawn from the essence of the Buddhadharma in all sutras. The Order does not uniquely follow the systematic arrangements of the Buddhist teachings proposed by any particular school. It seeks to realize the essence of the Dharma as it was in early Buddhism as well as the essence of the Dharma as it developed throughout history in all Buddhist traditions.

According to item five, the Order considers all sutras of the Buddhist canon, whether spoken by the Buddha or compiled later by Buddhist practitioners in the spirit of what the Buddha taught, as Buddhist sutras. The development of Original Buddhism into Schools' Buddhism was a necessary and genuine way of maintaining the spirit of Buddhism alive. Only by practicing and teaching in new ways, can Buddhist practitioners keep the vital spirit of Buddhism alive as an influence in the world.

In addition, the Charter addresses a willingness to be open and to change. It is expressed in item seven that the Order of Interbeing rejects dogmatic thinking and acting. It accepts versatile teachings and practices that reflect the progressive and relevant nature of Buddhism and which make it possible for the insight, compassion, and inclusiveness of Buddhism to be there in the heart of life. The Order considers the preservation of this spirit to be more important than the preservation of the outer forms and traditions of Buddhism. With the aspiration of a bodhisattva, members of the Order of Interbeing practice to transform their own habit energies in order to transform society in the way of compassion and understanding.

We can offer the insights of Buddhism to those who are pioneers in looking for ways to resolve the difficulties that they and society face.

The Charter of the Order of Interbeing (Tiep Hien)

Chapter I
Name, Aim, Tradition

1. A Buddhist community is formed with the name Order of Interbeing.

2. The aim of the Order is to actualize Buddhism by studying, experimenting with, and applying Buddhism in modern life, with a special emphasis on the bodhisattva ideal.

3. The Order of Interbeing was founded within the Linji School of Dhyana Buddhism. It is grounded in the Four Spirits: the spirit of nonattachment from views; the spirit of direct experimentation on the nature of interdependent origination through meditation; the spirit of appropriateness, and the spirit of Skillful Means. All four are to be found in all Buddhist traditions.

Chapter II
Basic Scriptures, Teachings, Methods

4. The Order of Interbeing does not consider any sutra or group of sutras as its basic scripture(s). It draws inspiration from the essence of the Buddhadharma in all sutras. It does not accept the systematic arrangements of the Buddhist teachings proposed by any school. The Order of Interbeing seeks to realize the spirit of the Dharma in early Buddhism, as well as in the development of that spirit through the history of the Sangha, and its life and teachings in all Buddhist traditions.

5. The Order of Interbeing considers all sutras, whether spoken by the Lord Buddha or compiled by later Buddhist generations, as Buddhist sutras. It is also able to find inspiration from the texts of other spiritual traditions. It considers the development of Original Buddhism into new schools a necessity to keep the spirit of Buddhism alive. Only by proposing new forms of Buddhist life can one help the true Buddhist spirit perpetuate.

6. The life of the Order of Interbeing should be nourished by understanding and compassion. Compassion and understanding, radiated by the Buddhist life, can contribute to the peace and happiness of humankind. The Order considers the principle of nonattachment from views and the principle of direct experimentation on interdependent origination through meditation to be the two most important guides for attaining true understanding. It considers the principle of appropriateness and the principle of Skillful Means as guides for actions in society. The spirit of nonattachment from views and the spirit of direct experimentation lead to open-mindedness and compassion, both in the realm of the perception of reality and in the realm of human relationships. The spirit of appropriateness and the spirit of Skillful Means lead to a capacity to be creative and to reconcile, both of which are necesary for the service of living beings.

7. The Order of Interbeing rejects dogmatism in both looking and acting. It seeks all forms of action that can revive and sustain the true spirit of insight and compassion in life. It considers this spirit to be more important than any Buddhist institution or tradition. With the aspiration of a bodhisattva, members of the Order of Interbeing seek to change themselves in order to change society in the direction of compassion and understanding by living a joyful and mindful life.

Chapter III
Authority, Membership, Organization

8. To protect and respect the freedom and responsibility of each member of the community, monks, nuns, and laypeople enjoy equality in the Order of Interbeing.

9. The Order of Interbeing does not recognize the necessity of a mediator between the Buddha and lay disciples, between humans and ultimate reality. It considers, however, the insight and experiences of ancestral teachers, monks, nuns, and laypeople, as helpful to those who are practicing the Way.

10. Members of the Order of Interbeing are either in the core community or the extended community. The core community consists of those who have made the commitment to observe the Fourteen Mindfulness Trainings of the Order and the Five Mindfulness Trainings, and who have been ordained as brothers and sisters in the Order. The extended community consists of members who, while trying to live the spirit of the Order of Interbeing, have not formally made the commitment to observe the Fourteen Mindfulness Trainings, nor received ordination in the Order of Interbeing. The members of the core community accept the responsibility to organize and support a local Sangha, and help sustain Mindfulness Training recitations, days of mindfulness, and mindfulness retreats.

11. The extended community lives in close relationship with the core community by attending the recitation of the Mindfulness Trainings every two weeks and by participating in spiritual and social events sponsored by the core community. Long-standing members of the extended community, those who have participated regularly for one year or more, should be consulted on an advisory basis on the applications of individuals to become members of the core community, whether or not these long-standing members of the extended community have received the Five Mindfulness Trainings.

12. *Dharmacharyas* (Dharma teachers) are members of the core community who have been selected as teachers based on their stability in the practice and ability to lead a happy life. They function to inspire joy and stability in the local Sanghas. Local Sanghas are encouraged to suggest potential Dharmacharyas.

Chapter IV
Mindfulness Trainings of the Order of Interbeing, Conditions for Ordination

13. The Mindfulness Trainings of the Order of Interbeing reflect the life of the Order, which considers spiritual practice as the base of all social action.

14. The Mindfulness Trainings are the heart of the Charter. Members are expected to recite the Five Mindfulness Trainings and the Fourteen Mindfulness Trainings every two weeks. If there is a three-month lapse in their recitation, their ordination is considered nullified.

15. All persons eighteen years old or older, regardless of race, nationality, color, gender, or sexual orientation, are eligible to join the Order if they have shown the capacity of learning and practicing the Mindfulness Trainings and other requirements of a core community member of the Order of Interbeing, and have formally received the Three Jewels and the Five Mindfulness Trainings.

16. A candidate begins the application process by announcing his or her aspiration to become a member of the core community of the Order of Interbeing. The announcement should be in writing to the local Sangha core community members, or if none are located nearby, to the appropriate Dharma teacher(s). A candidate must have received the Three Jewels and Five Mindfulness Trainings. One or more core community members shall then mentor and train the candidate for at least one year, until the candidate is happy and steadfast in the practice and practices in harmony with the Sangha. These steps enable the aspirant to get to know the core community better. Similarly, they enable the core community to get to know the aspirant better, to offer guidance and support, especially in areas of the practice where the aspirant may need additional guidance, and to train the aspirant in the role of Order member. When appropriate, the core community members and Dharma teachers(s) will decide, after making an advisory consultation with long-standing members of the extended community, whether or not that candidate is ready to receive ordination into the Order of Interbeing. The work of a core community Order member includes Sangha building and support, explaining the Dharma from personal experience, and nourishing the bodhichitta in others while maintaining a regular meditation practice in harmony and peace with one's family, all as manifestations of the bodhisattva ideal.

17. When the core community and the Dharma teacher(s) make a decision on an application, they will strive to use their Sangha eyes and take care to nourish the bodhichitta (mind of love) of the aspirant, even if a delay in ordination is suggested. Local Sanghas are authorized to embellish the application procedures in this Charter in a manner that reasonably addresses local culture, geography, and circumstances, provided that the goals and aspirations of the Order are not defeated. The application provisions set forth in the Charter respecting an individual's ordination may be waived in individual cases under special circumstances such as medical hardship, provided that, as appropriate, the coordinators of the Executive Council and most appropriate Dharma teacher(s) are consulted first, and, if time permits, the local or most appropriate core community members. When it has been indicated that the candidate is ready to receive the Order ordination, his or her name shall be reported to the person designated by the core community Assembly. When an ordination ceremony has taken place, it shall be declared in writing to the Secretary of the Order, giving the name, lineage name, and Dharma name of the ordinee; date and place of the ordination; and the name of the presiding Dharma teacher.

18. Members of the core community are expected to observe at least sixty days of mindfulness per year. It is recognized that this sixty-day requirement may be difficult for some members to achieve at times, due to family or other responsibilities, and the requirement is intended to be flexible in such cases, if it is agreed upon by the Sangha.

19. All members of the core community are expected to organize and practice with a local Sangha.

20. Provided they are consistent with the spirit of the Five Mindfulness Trainings and the Fourteen Mindfulness Trainings, all lifestyles (whether in a committed relationship or celibate) are considered equally valid for core community members. To support both partners in a relationship, it is helpful if the partner of a core community member is a member of the core community, a member of the extended community, or, at the minimum, that the member live in harmony with his or her partner and that the member's partner supports and encourages the member's practice.

Chapter V
Leadership, Community Properties, Accounting

21. At regular intervals, an Assembly of all core community members should gather for a council. All members shall be notified six months in advance of the date and location of the meeting. Any member unable to attend can appoint a proxy to speak for him or her. The process of consensus shall be presented, reviewed, and revised at the beginning of the meeting. Rotating teams of facilitators, one woman and one man, each of different nationality, shall conduct the meeting. Minutes of each meeting of the Assembly will be kept as an ongoing record of the life and work of the Order of Interbeing. They will be made available to members on request.

22. At the Assembly meeting, the core community will select members to serve on an Executive Council to organize and guide the work of the Order of Interbeing between Assemblies, and to approve coordinators of the Executive Council from among the members of the Executive Council. The Assembly will decide on the specific structure and organization that will best support the goals of reducing suffering, realizing the bodhisattva ideal, and maintaining a strong Sangha network. The core community will draw on the life maturity and practice maturity of its elders and on the freshness of its younger members for assistance and support, and encourage and benefit from an ongoing Council of Elders and Council of Youth.

23. In order to facilitate interaction with the worldwide Sangha, local Sanghas are encouraged to organize in a manner compatible with the spirit of this Charter.

24. To be a member of the Order core community, one is not required to pay financial dues, but dues may be suggested by the Executive Council and the Assembly as *dana* (donation) to support the work of the Order. All Order of Interbeing monies, including contributions and dues, are to be held in a separate fund under the name "Order of Interbeing." A detailed financial report prepared by the Treasurer(s) shall be presented to the membership annually. After administrative costs have been covered, funds of the Order may be used to help local Sanghas offer scholarships to members to attend Order retreats and in their work to relieve suffering.

25. Any community properties of the Order should be held under the national and local regulations of its site. To protect those who may be responsible for the management of community properties, all assets, including bank accounts, currency, real estate, vehicles, etc., are to be accounted for using common accounting practices. If and when local Sanghas hold funds for the international Order of Interbeing, accounting will be kept separately and detailed reports sent yearly to the Treasurer(s) of the Order.

Chapter VI
Amending of the Charter

26. Every word and every sentence in this Charter is subject to change, so that the spirit of the Charter will be allowed to remain alive throughout the history of the practice. Previous versions should be preserved and made available for consultation by later generations. All versions are to be clearly dated for future reference.

27. The Fourteen Mindfulness Trainings and this Charter are to be reexamined at each Assembly of the core community members.

28. The Charter, consisting of six chapters and twenty-nine items, should be revised and amended at each Assembly of the core community members in order to keep it relevant to today's societies.

29. In keeping with the tradition of the Sangha, all changes must be made by consensus and not just by simple majority.

The Community of Interbeing and the Order Member

The Order of Interbeing consists of a core community and an extended community. The core community is composed of members who have made the formal commitment in front of the Sangha to practice the Fourteen Mindfulness Trainings of the Order. The extended community consists of those who attempt to live up to the spirit of the Order, but who have not formally made this commitment. Members of the extended community cooperate closely with core community members in all activities, including the recitation of the Fourteen Mindfulness Trainings. To become a member of the core community, a person undergoes an apprenticeship of one or more years, under the supervision of one or more mentors, and practices with members of the core community. After the ceremony for receiving the Fourteen Mindfulness Trainings, he or she agrees to observe at least sixty days of mindfulness a year.

Only when you have the feeling that you have enough time, energy, and interest to take care of a community, and you have your Sangha's support, should you ask for formal ordination. Then you will be working together with other brothers and sisters to help build community.

An Order member should be a pillar, a source of inspiration. The brown jacket of the Order member is a symbol of humility. Brown is the color of the earth and of the peasants' clothes in Vietnam. So when we put on the brown jacket, we must be humble. Brown also represents a silent, inner strength, which though silent, is very powerful. Whether we wear the brown robe of a monk or the brown jacket of a lay practitioner, we need to represent the virtues of humility and silent strength. We do not consider ourselves to be better than others or to have more authority.

As an Order member, we have many things to take care of, and everything we do is done in the spirit of practice. We see the Buddha, the Dharma, and the Sangha as the object of our practice, and working for them brings us much joy. We need to have the energy and the vitality that come from practicing the right Dharma. Even in my eighties I find much joy in translating the sutras, teaching, practicing, walking mindfully, and leading people in the practice in many different countries all over the world. If we feel we lack the energy, it is because we lack the strength of a deep aspiration. We have to be highly motivated to do the work of the Buddha, the Dharma, and the Sangha for others, for our ancestors, and for our society. We have an ideal, a strength born of our deep aspiration and faith. An Order member should have a fire in their heart that drives them forward. Our purpose is not to acquire fame, profit, or a high position but to cultivate the great love that will make us a worthy continuation of the Buddha, our ancestral teachers, and of Thầy.

If we have received the lamp of Dharma transmission or are an aspirant Dharma teacher, we do not study Buddhism in order to show off our knowledge of Buddhism in a Dharma sharing or a Dharma talk. We just speak about and give instruction on what we are truly practicing. If we teach walking meditation it means we have accomplished the practice of walking meditation to a significant extent. If not, we should not teach it; we should take more time to practice it. The expression 身教 means we teach with our physical presence, with our life. There are those who do not like giving Dharma talks and yet they are excellent Dharma teachers, because when they walk, stand, sit, or lie down, they do so with mindfulness; and they know how to engage and live with others in harmony, with peace, joy, and openness. Theirs is a living Dharma talk. Such people are precious gems in the Sangha, whether they are monks, nuns, or laypeople.

There are many accomplished lay practitioners who are very learned but still practice humbly and unostentatiously. Throughout the history of Buddhism in Vietnam, many such lay Dharma teachers have earned the respect and admiration of monks and nuns who regarded them as their teacher. Thiều

Chửu (1902–1954), author of a Chinese-Vietnamese dictionary, and Tâm Minh Lê Đình Thám (1897–1969) are examples of lay Dharma teachers whose practice was extremely solid. They would ascend the Dharma platform and teach sutras to monks and nuns and would do so with a great deal of humility. Whenever the layman Lê Đình Thám came up to teach the monks and nuns, he always wore the customary temple robe for laypeople and prostrated before the monks and nuns before ascending the Dharma throne. The monks and nuns had a great deal of respect for him because he practiced what he taught.

In principle there is no hindrance, no barrier separating monastic and lay practitioners, because the aspiration of all of us is to bring Buddhism into the world and to do this together, to make Buddhism a reality that can be applied in any situation. The world really needs Dharma teachers. The monks and nuns also go out into the world to teach but the number of monastic Dharma teachers is not enough to meet the demand, which is why we need many many more lay Dharma teachers. In Europe, for example, almost every country wants to have a retreat every year, but if we were to satisfy all the demands, there would be no one left in Plum Village to take care of the practice at home.

We need to have strong residential Sanghas as bases, such as Plum Village in France, the EIAB in Germany, Blue Cliff, Deer Park, and Magnolia Grove in the US, Plum Village Thailand, or other Plum Village practice centers around the world, which always need to have a stable Fourfold Sangha all year round as a resource.[20] Only a limited number of monastics can go out to teach at one time. The rest need to stay home to take care of the center and its guests. However the lay order members, as the long arm of the Fourfold Sangha, can more readily reach out into society to transmit the teachings and share the practice.

We need thousands of lay Order members to do the necessary work of bringing the teachings of transformation and healing into the world. Of course they are not expected to be professors of Buddhist Studies. They organize the practice and they are exemplars of the practice. They have to master the Dharma doors of Applied Buddhism, touching happiness as they sit in meditation, take each step in mindfulness, or practice noble silence. They have the capacity to organize a local Sangha in which all the members practice together happily and in harmony. A Sangha needs brotherhood and sisterhood in order to be a source of trust and refuge for people, both at a local and national level. What is most important as an Order member is not whether or not you have authority or whether or not you are a Dharma teacher. What is most important is that you practice in such a way that you help create a Sangha where you live, in which everyone practices together happily, where everyone looks on the others as their own brothers and sisters, members of one spiritual family, a

[20] The Sangha that consists of monks, nuns, laymen and laywomen.

local Sangha where no one craves authority, power, or attention, where no one is more important than the other, and where everyone knows how to use loving speech and listen to each other deeply. In every country, in every city we need Sanghas like that: in London, Tokyo, New York, Mexico City, Sydney, Gaborone, and Bangkok to name but a few. Who is going to do this? The lay Order members. The monks and nuns will give support and sometimes we shall do it together, but the lay Order members are the people chiefly responsible for setting up these Sanghas.

We need to build a Sangha, mindfulness hub, or practice center where we live, and to be successful we need to be able to work collaboratively, to have the ability to let go of our views, to be open to the input of others, and to embrace and love those around us without striving for any special recognition, position, authority, or personal advantage. This is something the monks, nuns, and lay practitioners are already doing, and we can do even better in the future. If we are united in this mission, if we are in harmony with each other, if there is brotherhood, sisterhood, and happiness, then the positive effects of our Sangha building will spread far and wide, and Thầy will also feel these beneficial effects. This is how to make Thầy happy.

When the lay Order of Interbeing has happiness, it is very easy to work along with the monastic Sangha in harmony. Everyone has their own talents, virtues, and qualities, and the Sangha will recognize these and invite everyone to do the kind of work that matches their skills and meets the Sangha's needs. We have lay Dharma teachers, lay Dharma teacher aspirants, and many other lay practitioners who are practicing well. They work quietly and selflessly without trying to attract attention. They organize retreats, Days of Mindfulness, and give wonderful Dharma talks and instruction in the practice. People such as these do not create conflicts in the Sangha. On the contrary, they bring happiness to many people. We hope that in the future we shall have longer retreats for members of the Order of Interbeing in which the Order members are able to consolidate and deepen their practice, their aspirations and happiness, and fulfill the responsibility that the Buddha and the ancestral teachers have entrusted to them. We have to receive and realize that aspiration and make it become reality.

If our local Sangha is still in disorder, if the members cannot sit down together happily, if they do not have enough love for each other and cannot work together, then we have not yet succeeded in our task. As members of the Order this is our responsibility. We cannot blame others for the difficulties that have arisen. We have to see that it is because our practice is still imperfect, we are not solid or humble enough, and we do not have enough silent inner strength.

Guidelines for Receiving the Fourteen Mindfulness Trainings

Sister Chân Không, Plum Village 2015

In the beginning Thay always chose personally those who were to receive the Fourteen Mindfulness Trainings but for many years now it has been the local Sanghas, Order Members, and Dharma teachers who choose who is to receive them. The process differs a little from country to country, but broadly speaking without the acceptance of the core community of their own country, their mentor(s), and their local Sangha, a person cannot receive the trainings. It depends on the previous years of mentorship as to whether a person can receive the trainings or not. Someone who wishes to receive the trainings will have already received and been practicing the Five Mindfulness Trainings for two years.[21] They will write a letter addressed to Thay requesting to become an aspirant to receive the trainings and send it to their national Sangha of core OI members. If the request is accepted, they will

[21] This is an update that can be incorporated into the revision of the Charter.

receive one or more mentors who will guide them in regular meetings in the practice of being a core member and the Fourteen Trainings. During the time of aspirancy they attend Days of Mindfulness and retreats with their local and national Sanghas. After at least one year of mentorship, if their mentor sees they are ready, they can apply to receive the trainings in a ceremony that is organized at one of the Plum Village monasteries or in a retreat elsewhere in which at least four Dharma teachers are present. Normally at least two of these should be monastic Dharma teachers.

Although Thay does not transmit the trainings personally, he is understood to be the transmission master, and the four Dharma teachers are only representing Thay. This is stated clearly on the Mindfulness Trainings certificate, which is handed to the ordinees at the ceremony. Before the ordination the aspirant makes an application that contains a letter from the aspirant describing their deep aspiration to be a core member, a letter of support from all the core members of their local Sangha, and a letter of support from their mentor(s). A copy of this application is sent to the monastic Dharma teachers who will lead the ceremony as well as to the appropriate OI representative in their own country. In order to avoid two core members having the same Dharma name, all Dharma names must come from or have the approval of the presiding Secretary of the Order, currently Sister Chân Không. Before the aspirant can be given a Dharma name, Sister Chân Không or her assistant, currently Sister Định Nghiêm, needs to be informed of the surname, forename, lineage name received when taking the Five Mindfulness Trainings, letter of aspiration, name and country of local Sangha, email address of the aspirant, place of ordination, and date of ordination. It is easiest if the monastic Dharma teachers leading the ceremony can inform Sister Chân Không.

Part Four

Ceremonies

Reciting the Mindfulness Trainings

The Fourteen Mindfulness Trainings are recited at least once every two weeks. Usually, a member of the core community is asked to lead the recitation. However, a member of the extended community can also be invited to lead as long as they are familiar with the ceremony, have a solid presence, and enjoy the respect of the community.[22]

Participants sit in two or more rows facing each other. The person who sits nearest the altar in the row on the right as you face the altar, is called the "head of the ceremony." This person leads the ceremony and is responsible for inviting the bell, and for announcing the Sanghakarman Procedure. Two people sitting on opposite sides should be chosen to perform the Sanghakarman Procedure, and either one or two people should be chosen to recite the trainings. The recitation should be neither too slow nor too quick, as the right speed will

[22] When monks and nuns are present they will lead the ceremony unless they specifically ask laypeople to do so.

please the community. The leader of the recitation should be visible to everyone.

At the beginning of the ceremony, someone who has the capacity to do so offers incense and leads the chanting of the incense offering verse. The rest of the community is standing and, with palms joined, follows their breathing. The incense offering is followed by Invoking the Names of the Buddhas, Bodhisattvas, and Ancestral Teachers. After each name is invoked, everyone touches the earth together. Then the members of the community sit down. When everyone is completely settled, the bell is invited to sound, and the recitation begins with Praising the Buddha, the Sutra Opening Verse and the recitation of the sutra The Insight that Brings Us to the Other Shore. Then follows the Sanghakarman Procedure, in which it is confirmed that there is harmony in the Community, that everyone is present, and that today is the agreed date for reciting the Fourteen Mindfulness Trainings.[23]

From the very beginning of the ceremony, everyone follows their breathing and practices mindfulness. Whether listening, chanting, joining palms, bowing, touching the earth, sitting down, or even adjusting posture, there is an appropriate verse for each movement to help us be more mindful in our actions.[24]

---

[23] For these verses see Thich Nhat Hanh: *Chanting from the Heart*, Parallax, 2007.

[24] For these verses see Thich Nhat Hanh: *Present Moment, Wonderful Moment: Mindfulness Verses for Daily Living*, Parallax, 2002.

During the recitation, each member of the community should give full attention to the Mindfulness Training being read in order to receive and reflect on its content. Concentrating on the trainings this way will keep the mind free of distracting thoughts. The person who recites them should speak in a clear voice that communicates the spirit of the trainings. The community's successful concentration depends on the quality of the reading.

Before reading out the trainings, the reader begins by asking, "Brothers and Sisters, are you ready?" and each person answers silently, "I am ready." After reciting each Training, the reader will take a breath before asking, "This is the (First) Mindfulness Training of the Order of Interbeing. Have you studied, practiced, and observed it during the past two weeks?" and then pause for the length of three breaths, in and out. This pause allows everyone to dwell on the essence and the content of the Training. The answer to the question falls somewhere between yes and no. Everyone who practices mindfulness and follows the trainings is entitled to say yes; it would be wrong to say no. But our yes may not be 100 percent, because our efforts during the past two weeks may not have been enough. So our answer may be something like, "Yes, but I could have done better." We should allow time for the question to penetrate deep into our heart and mind and act on us during the silence of the three breaths. While allowing the question to penetrate, we can follow our breathing attentively. The head of ceremony should observe three mindful breaths before inviting the bell to sound. When the bell sounds, the entire community joins their palms, and the reader proceeds to the next Mindfulness Training. During this time of breathing, if anyone has a copy of the text of the ceremony, they should refrain from touching or turning the page until the bell sounds. Practicing in this way creates a serene atmosphere.

Recitation of the Fourteen Mindfulness Trainings

Sitting Meditation

Incense Offering

Touching the Earth

Sutra Opening Verse

Namo Tassa Bhagavato Arahato Samma Sambuddhassa (x3)

[Bell]

The Dharma is deep and lovely.
We now have a chance to see,
study, and to practice it.
We vow to realize its true meaning.

[Bell]

The Insight that Brings Us to the Other Shore

Avalokiteshvara, while practicing deeply
with the Insight that Brings Us to the Other Shore,
suddenly discovered that all of the five Skandhas
are equally empty, and with this realization
he overcame all Ill-being. [Bell]

"Listen Sariputra, this Body itself is Emptiness
and Emptiness itself is this Body.
This Body is not other than Emptiness
and Emptiness is not other than this Body.
The same is true of Feelings, Perceptions,
Mental Formations, and Consciousness. [Bell]

Listen Sariputra, all phenomena bear the mark of Emptiness;
their true nature is the nature of no Birth no Death,
no Being no Nonbeing, no Defilement no Purity,
no Increasing no Decreasing.
That is why in Emptiness, Body, Feelings,
Perceptions, Mental Formations, and Consciousness
are not separate self entities.
The Eighteen Realms of Phenomena,
which are the six Sense Organs,
Six Sense Objects, and six Consciousnesses
are also not separate self entities.
The Twelve Links of Interdependent Arising
and their Extinction are also not separate self entities.

Ill-being, the Causes of Ill-being, the End of Ill-being,
the Path, insight, and attainment,
are also not separate self entities.
Whoever can see this no longer needs anything to attain. [Bell]

Bodhisattvas who practice
the Insight that Brings Us to the Other Shore
see no more obstacles in their mind,
and because there are no more obstacles in their mind,
they can overcome all fear, destroy all wrong perceptions,
and realize Perfect Nirvana. [Bell]

All Buddhas in the past, present, and future
by practicing the Insight that Brings Us to the Other Shore
are all capable of attaining Authentic
and Perfect Enlightenment. [Bell]

Therefore Sariputra, it should be known that
the Insight that Brings Us to the Other Shore
is a Great Mantra, the most illuminating mantra,
the highest mantra, a mantra beyond compare,
the True Wisdom that has the power
to put an end to all kinds of suffering.
Therefore let us proclaim a mantra to praise
the Insight that Brings Us to the Other Shore.

Gate, Gate, Paragate, Parasamgate, Bodhi Svaha! (x3)
[Bell x2]

Sanghakarman Procedure

Sanghakarman Master: Has the community of the Order of Interbeing assembled?

Sangha Convener: Yes, the community of the Order of Interbeing has assembled.

Sanghakarman Master: Is there harmony in the community?

Sangha Convener: Yes, there is harmony.

Sanghakarman Master: Is there anyone not able to be present who has asked to be represented and have they declared themselves to have done their best to study and practice the Mindfulness Trainings?

Sangha Convener: No, there is not.

OR

Sangha Convener: Yes, [name], for health reasons, cannot be at the recitation today. They have asked [name] to represent them and they declare that they have done their best to study and practice the Mindfulness Trainings.

Sanghakarman Master: Why has the community assembled today?

Sangha Convener: The community has assembled to practice the recitation of the Fourteen Mindfulness Trainings of the Order of Interbeing.

Sanghakarman Master: Noble community of the Order of Interbeing, please listen. Today, [date], has been declared as the day to recite the Fourteen Mindfulness Training of the Order of Interbeing. The community has assembled at the appointed time and is ready to hear and to recite the Mindfulness Trainings in an atmosphere of harmony. Thus, the recitation can proceed. Is this statement clear and complete?

Everyone: Clear and complete.

[Bell]

Reciting the Fourteen Mindfulness Trainings

Dear Sangha, this is the moment when we enjoy reciting the Fourteen Mindfulness Trainings of the Order of Interbeing. The Fourteen Mindfulness Trainings are the very essence of the Order of Interbeing. They are the torch lighting our path, the boat carrying us, the teacher guiding us. They allow us to touch the nature of interbeing in everything that is and to see that our happiness is not separate from the happiness of others. Interbeing is not a theory; it is a reality that can be directly experienced by each of us at any moment in our daily lives. The Fourteen Mindfulness Trainings help us cultivate concentration and insight, which free us from fear and the illusion of a separate self. Please listen to each mindfulness training with a serene mind. The Mindfulness Trainings serve as a clear mirror in which to look at ourselves. Say "yes," silently, every time you see that you have made an effort to study, practice, and observe the Mindfulness Training read.

These, then, are the Fourteen Mindfulness Trainings of the Order of Interbeing.

The First Mindfulness Training
Openness

Aware of the suffering created by fanaticism and intolerance, we are determined not to be idolatrous about or bound to any doctrine, theory, or ideology, even Buddhist ones. We are committed to seeing the Buddhist teachings as a guiding means that help us learn to look deeply and develop understanding and compassion. They are not doctrines to fight, kill, or die for. We understand that fanaticism in its many forms is the result of perceiving things in a dualistic and discriminative manner. We will train ourselves to look at everything with openness and the insight of interbeing in order to transform dogmatism and violence in ourselves and the world.

This is the First Mindfulness Training of the Order of Interbeing. Have we made an effort to study, practice, and observe it during the past two weeks? (3 breaths)

[Bell]

The Second Mindfulness Training
Nonattachment to Views

Aware of the suffering created by attachment to views and wrong perceptions, we are determined to avoid being narrow-minded and bound to present views. We are committed to learning and practicing nonattachment to views and being open to others' insights and experiences in order to benefit from the collective wisdom. Insight is revealed through the practice of compassionate listening, deep looking, and letting go of notions rather than through the accumulation of intellectual knowledge. We are aware that the knowledge we presently possess is not changeless, absolute truth. Truth is found in life and we will observe life within and around us in every moment, ready to learn throughout our lives.

This is the Second Mindfulness Training of the Order of Interbeing. Have we made an effort to study, practice, and observe it during the past two weeks? (3 breaths)

[Bell]

The Third Mindfulness Training
Freedom of Thought

Aware of the suffering brought about when we impose our views on others, we are determined not to force others, even our children, by any means whatsoever—such as authority, threat, money, propaganda, or indoctrination—to adopt our views. We are committed to respecting the right of others to be different, to choose what to believe and how to decide. We will, however, learn to help others let go of and transform fanaticism and narrowness through loving speech and compassionate dialogue.

This is the Third Mindfulness Training of the Order of Interbeing. Have we made an effort to study, practice, and observe it during the past two weeks? (3 breaths)

[Bell]

The Fourth Mindfulness Training
Awareness of Suffering

Aware that looking deeply at the nature of suffering can help us develop understanding and compassion, we are determined to come home to ourselves, to recognize, accept, embrace, and listen to our own suffering with the energy of mindfulness. We will do our best not to run away from our suffering or cover it up through consumption, but practice conscious breathing and walking to look deeply into the roots of our suffering. We know we can only find the path leading to the transformation of suffering when we understand the roots of our suffering. Once we have understood our own suffering, we will be able to understand the suffering of others. We are committed to finding ways, including personal contact and using telephone, electronic, audio-visual and other means, to be with those who suffer, so we can help them transform their suffering into compassion, peace and joy.

This is the Fourth Mindfulness Training of the Order of Interbeing. Have we made an effort to study, practice, and observe it during the past two weeks? (3 breaths)

[Bell]

The Fifth Mindfulness Training
Compassionate, Healthy Living

Aware that true happiness is rooted in peace, solidity, freedom and compassion, we are determined not to accumulate wealth while millions are hungry and dying, nor to take as the aim of our life fame, power, wealth or sensual pleasure, which can bring much suffering and despair. We will practice looking deeply into how we nourish our body and mind with edible foods, sense impressions, volition and consciousness. We are committed not to gamble or to use alcohol, drugs, or any other products which bring toxins into our own and the collective body and consciousness such as certain websites, electronic games, TV programs, films, magazines, books, and conversations. We will consume in a way that preserves compassion, well-being, and joy in our bodies and consciousness and in the collective body and consciousness of our families, our society, and the Earth.

This is the Fifth Mindfulness Trainings of the Order of Interbeing. Have we made an effort to study, practice and observe it during the past two weeks? (3 breaths)

[Bell]

The Sixth Mindfulness Training
Taking Care of Anger

Aware that anger blocks communication and creates suffering, we are committed to taking care of our energy of anger when it arises, and to recognizing and transforming the seeds of anger that lie deep in our consciousness. When anger manifests, we are determined not to do or say anything, but to practice mindful breathing or mindful walking to acknowledge, embrace, and look deeply into our anger. We know that the roots of anger are not outside of ourselves but can be found in our wrong perceptions and lack of understanding of the suffering in ourselves and others. By contemplating impermanence, we will be able to look with the eyes of compassion at ourselves and at those we think are the cause of our anger, and to recognize the preciousness of our relationships. We will practice Right Diligence in order to nourish our capacity of understanding, love, joy and inclusiveness, gradually transforming our anger, violence, and fear and helping others do the same.

This is the Sixth Mindfulness Training of the Order of Interbeing. Have we made an effort to study, practice, and observe it during the past two weeks? (3 breaths)

[Bell]

The Seventh Mindfulness Training
Dwelling Happily in the Present Moment

Aware that life is available only in the present moment, we are committed to training ourselves to live deeply each moment of daily life. We will try not to lose ourselves in dispersion or be carried away by regrets about the past, worries about the future, or craving, anger, or jealousy in the present. We will practice mindful breathing to be aware of what is happening in the here and now.

We are determined to learn the art of mindful living by touching the wondrous, refreshing, and healing elements that are inside and around us, in all situations. In this way, we will be able to cultivate seeds of joy, peace, love and understanding in ourselves, thus facilitating the work of transformation and healing in our consciousness. We are aware that real happiness depends primarily on our mental attitude and not on external conditions and that we can live happily in the present moment simply by remembering that we already have more than enough conditions to be happy.

This is the Seventh Mindfulness Training of the Order of Interbeing. Have we made an effort to study, practice, and observe it during the past two weeks? (3 breaths)

[Bell]

The Eighth Mindfulness Training
True Community and Communication

Aware that lack of communication always brings separation and suffering, we are committed to training ourselves in the practice of compassionate listening and loving speech. Knowing that true community is rooted in inclusiveness and in the concrete practice of the harmony of views, thinking, and speech, we will practice to share our understanding and experiences with members in our community in order to arrive at collective insight. We are determined to learn to listen deeply without judging or reacting, and refrain from uttering words that can create discord or cause the community to break. Whenever difficulties arise, we will remain in our Sangha and practice looking deeply into ourselves and others to recognize all the causes and conditions, including our own habit energies, that have brought about the difficulties. We will take responsibility for all the ways we may have contributed to the conflict and keep communication open. We will not behave as a victim but be active in finding ways to reconcile and resolve all conflicts, however small.

This is the Eighth Mindfulness Training of the Order of Interbeing. Have we made an effort to study, practice, and observe it during the past two weeks? (3 breaths)

[Bell]

The Ninth Mindfulness Training
Truthful and Loving Speech

Aware that words can create happiness or suffering, we are committed to learning to speak truthfully, lovingly, and constructively. We will use only words that inspire joy, confidence, and hope as well as promote reconciliation and peace in ourselves and among other people. We will speak and listen in a way that can help ourselves and others to transform suffering and see the way out of difficult situations. We are determined not to say untruthful things for the sake of personal interest or to impress people, nor to utter words that might cause division or hatred. We will protect the happiness and harmony of our Sangha by refraining from speaking about the faults of other persons in their absence and always ask ourselves whether our perceptions are correct. We will speak only with the intention to understand and help transform the situation. We will not spread rumors nor criticize or condemn things of which we are not sure. We will do our best to speak out about situations of injustice, even when doing so may make difficulties for us or threaten our safety.

This is the Ninth Mindfulness Training of the Order of Interbeing. Have we made an effort to study, practice, and observe it during the past two weeks? (3 breaths)

[Bell]

The Tenth Mindfulness Training
Protecting and Nourishing the Sangha

Aware that the essence and aim of a Sangha is the practice of understanding and compassion, we are determined not to use the Buddhist community for personal power or profit, or transform our community into a political instrument. As members of a spiritual community, we should nonetheless take a clear stand against oppression and injustice. We should strive to change the situation, without taking sides in a conflict. We are committed to learning to look with the eyes of interbeing and to see ourselves and others as cells in one Sangha body. As a true cell in the Sangha body, generating mindfulness, concentration, and insight to nourish ourselves and the whole community, each of us is at the same time a cell in the Buddha body. We will actively build brotherhood and sisterhood, flow as a river, and practice to develop the three real powers—understanding, love, and cutting through afflictions—to realize collective awakening.

This is the Tenth Mindfulness Training of the Order of Interbeing. Have we made an effort to study, practice, and observe it during the past two weeks? (3 breaths)

[Bell]

The Eleventh Mindfulness Training
Right Livelihood

Aware that great violence and injustice have been done to our environment and society, we are committed not to live with a vocation that is harmful to humans and nature. We will do our best to select a livelihood that contributes to the well-being of all species on Earth and helps realize our ideal of understanding and compassion. Aware of economic, political, and social realities around the world, as well as our interrelationship with the ecosystem, we are determined to behave responsibly as consumers and as citizens. We will not invest in or purchase from companies that contribute to the depletion of natural resources, harm the Earth, or deprive others of their chance to live.

This is the Eleventh Mindfulness Training of the Order of Interbeing. Have we made an effort to study, practice, and observe it during the past two weeks? (3 breaths)

[Bell]

The Twelfth Mindfulness Training
Reverence for Life

Aware that much suffering is caused by war and conflict, we are determined to cultivate nonviolence, compassion, and the insight of interbeing in our daily lives and promote peace education, mindful mediation, and reconciliation within families, communities, ethnic and religious groups, nations, and in the world. We are committed not to kill and not to let others kill. We will not support any act of killing in the world, in our thinking, or in our way of life. We will diligently practice deep looking with our Sangha to discover better ways to protect life, prevent war, and build peace.

This is the Twelfth Mindfulness Training of the Order of Interbeing. Have we made an effort to study, practice, and observe it during the past two weeks? (3 breaths)

[Bell]

The Thirteenth Mindfulness Training
Generosity

Aware of the suffering caused by exploitation, social injustice, stealing, and oppression, we are committed to cultivating generosity in our way of thinking, speaking, and acting. We will practice loving kindness by working for the happiness of people, animals, plants, and minerals, and sharing our time, energy, and material resources with those who are in need. We are determined not to steal and not to possess anything that should belong to others. We will respect the property of others, but will try to prevent others from profiting from human suffering or the suffering of other beings.

This is the Thirteenth Mindfulness Training of the Order of Interbeing. Have we made an effort to study, practice, and observe it during the past two weeks? (3 breaths)

[Bell]

The Fourteenth Mindfulness Training
True Love

For lay members: Aware that sexual desire is not love and that sexual relations motivated by craving cannot dissipate the feeling of loneliness but will create more suffering, frustration, and isolation, we are determined not to engage in sexual relations without mutual understanding, love, and a deep long-term commitment. We resolve to find spiritual support for the integrity of our relationships from family members, friends, and sangha with whom there is support and trust. We know that to preserve the happiness of ourselves and others, we must respect the rights and commitments of ourselves and others. Recognizing the diversity of human experience, we are committed not to discriminate against any form of gender identity or sexual orientation. Seeing that body and mind are interrelated, we are committed to learning appropriate ways to take care of our sexual energy and cultivating loving kindness, compassion, joy, and inclusiveness for our own happiness and the happiness of others. We must be aware of future suffering that may be caused by sexual relations. We will treat our bodies with compassion and respect. We are determined to look deeply into the Four Nutriments and learn ways to preserve and channel our vital energies (sexual, breath, spirit) for the realization of our bodhisattva ideal. We will do everything in our power to protect children from sexual abuse and to prevent couples and families from being broken by sexual misconduct. We will be fully aware of the responsibility of bringing new lives into the world and will meditate regularly upon their future environment.

For monastic members: Aware that the deep aspiration of a monk or a nun can only be realized when he or she wholly leaves behind the bonds of sensual love, we are committed to practicing chastity and to helping others protect themselves. We are aware that loneliness and suffering cannot be alleviated through a sexual relationship, but through practicing loving kindness, compassion, joy, and inclusiveness. We know that a sexual relationship will destroy our monastic life, will prevent us from realizing our ideal of serving living beings, and will harm others. We will learn appropriate ways to take care of our sexual energy. We are determined not to suppress or mistreat our body or look upon our body as only an instrument, but will learn to handle our body with compassion and respect. We will look deeply into the Four Nutriments in order to preserve and channel our vital energies (sexual, breath, spirit) for the realization of our bodhisattva ideal.

This is the Fourteenth Mindfulness Training of the Order of Interbeing. Have we made an effort to study, practice, and observe it during the past two weeks? (3 breaths)

[Bell]

Concluding Words

Brothers and sisters, we have recited the Fourteen Mindfulness Trainings of the Order of Interbeing as the community has wished. We thank all of our sisters and brothers for helping us to do it serenely.

[Bell]

Sharing the Merit

Reciting the trainings, practicing the way of awareness
gives rise to benefits without limit.
We vow to share the fruit with all beings.
We vow to offer tribute to parents, teachers,
friends, and numerous beings
who give guidance and support along the path.

[Bell x3]

Recitation of the Five Mindfulness Trainings

Incense Offering

Touching the Earth

Sutra Opening Verse

The Insight that Brings Us to the Other Shore

Sanghakarman Procedure

Sanghakarman Master: Has the entire community assembled?

Sanghakarman Convener: The entire community has assembled.

Sanghakarman Master: Is there harmony in the community?

Sanghakarman Convener: Yes, there is harmony.

Sanghakarman Master: Is there anyone not able to be present who has asked to be represented, and have they declared themselves to have done their best to study and practice the Five Mindfulness Trainings?

Sanghakarman Convener: No, there is not.

OR

Sangha Convener: Yes, [name], for health reasons, cannot be at the recitation today. They have asked [name] to represent them and they declare that they have done their best to study and practice the Mindfulness Trainings.

Sanghakarman Master: What is the reason for the community gathering today?

Sanghakarman Convener: The community has gathered to practice the recitation of the Five Mindfulness Trainings.

Sanghakarman Master: Noble community, please listen. Today, [date], has been declared to be the Mindfulness Training Recitation Day. We have gathered at the appointed time. The noble community is ready to hear and recite the Mindfulness Trainings in an atmosphere of harmony, and the recitation can proceed. Is this statement clear and complete?

Everyone: Clear and complete

[Bell]

Introductory Words

Dear Sangha, this is the moment when we enjoy reciting the Five Mindfulness Trainings together. The Five Mindfulness Trainings represent the Buddhist vision for a global spirituality and ethic. They are a concrete expression of the Buddha's teachings on the Four Noble Truths and the Noble Eightfold Path, the path of right understanding and true love, leading to healing, transformation, and happiness for ourselves and for the world. To practice the Five Mindfulness Trainings is to cultivate the insight of interbeing, or Right View, which can remove all discrimination, intolerance, anger, fear, and despair. If we live according to the Five Mindfulness Trainings, we are already on the path of a bodhisattva. Knowing we are on this path, we are not lost in confusion about our life in the present or in fears about the future.

Please listen to each Mindfulness Training with a serene mind. Breathe mindfully and answer "yes" silently every time you see that you have made an effort to study, practice, and observe the mindfulness training read.

The Five Mindfulness Trainings

The First Mindfulness Training
Reverence for Life

Aware of the suffering caused by the destruction of life, I am committed to cultivating the insight of interbeing and compassion and learning ways to protect the lives of people, animals, plants, and minerals. I am determined not to kill, not to let others kill, and not to support any act of killing in the world, in my thinking, or in my way of life. Seeing that harmful actions arise from anger, fear, greed, and intolerance, which in turn come from dualistic and discriminative thinking, I will cultivate openness, nondiscrimination, and nonattachment to views in order to transform violence, fanaticism, and dogmatism in myself and in the world.

This is the first of the Five Mindfulness Trainings. Have you made an effort to study, practice, and observe it during the past two weeks? (3 breaths)

[Bell]

The Second Mindfulness Training
True Happiness

Aware of the suffering caused by exploitation, social injustice, stealing, and oppression, I am committed to practicing generosity in my thinking, speaking, and acting. I am determined not to steal and not to possess anything that should belong to others; and I will share my time, energy, and material resources with those who are in need. I will practice looking deeply to see that the happiness and suffering of others are not separate from my own happiness and suffering; that true happiness is not possible without understanding and compassion; and that running after wealth, fame, power, and sensual pleasures can bring much suffering and despair. I am aware that happiness depends on my mental attitude and not on external conditions, and that I can live happily in the present moment simply by remembering that I already have more than enough conditions to be happy. I am committed to practicing Right Livelihood so that I can help reduce the suffering of living beings on Earth and stop contributing to climate change.

This is the second of the Five Mindfulness Trainings. Have you made an effort to study, practice, and observe it during the past two weeks? (3 breaths)

[Bell]

The Third Mindfulness Training
True Love

Aware of the suffering caused by sexual misconduct, I am committed to cultivating responsibility and learning ways to protect the safety and integrity of individuals, couples, families, and society. Knowing that sexual desire is not love, and that sexual activity motivated by craving always harms myself as well as others, I am determined not to engage in sexual relations without mutual consent, true love, and a deep long-term commitment. I resolve to find spiritual support for the integrity of my relationship from family members, friends, and sangha with whom there is support and trust. I will do everything in my power to protect children from sexual abuse and to prevent couples and families from being broken by sexual misconduct. Seeing that body and mind are interrelated, I am committed to learn appropriate ways to take care of my sexual energy and to cultivate the four basic elements of true love—loving kindness, compassion, joy, and inclusiveness—for the greater happiness of myself and others. Recognizing the diversity of human experience, I am committed not to discriminate against any form of gender identity or sexual orientation. Practicing true love, we know that we will continue beautifully into the future.

This is the third of the Five Mindfulness Trainings. Have you made an effort to study, practice, and observe it during the past two weeks? (3 breaths)

[Bell]

The Fourth Mindfulness Training
Loving Speech and Deep Listening

Aware of the suffering caused by unmindful speech and the inability to listen to others, I am committed to cultivating loving speech and compassionate listening in order to relieve suffering and to promote reconciliation and peace in myself and among other people, ethnic and religious groups, and nations. Knowing that words can create happiness or suffering, I am committed to speaking truthfully using words that inspire confidence, joy, and hope. When anger is manifesting in me, I am determined not to speak. I will practice mindful breathing and walking in order to recognize and to look deeply into my anger. I know that the roots of anger can be found in my wrong perceptions and lack of understanding of the suffering in myself and in the other person. I will speak and listen in a way that can help myself and the other person to transform suffering and see the way out of difficult situations. I am determined not to spread news that I do not know to be certain and not to utter words that can cause division or discord. I will practice Right Diligence to nourish my capacity for understanding, love, joy, and inclusiveness, and gradually transform anger, violence, and fear that lie deep in my consciousness.

This is the fourth of the Five Mindfulness Trainings. Have you made an effort to study, practice, and observe it during the past two weeks? (3 breaths)

[Bell]

The Fifth Mindfulness Training
Nourishment and Healing

Aware of the suffering caused by unmindful consumption, I am committed to cultivating good health, both physical and mental, for myself, my family, and my society by practicing mindful eating, drinking, and consuming. I will practice looking deeply into how I consume the Four Kinds of Nutriments, namely edible foods, sense impressions, volition, and consciousness. I am determined not to gamble or to use alcohol, drugs, or any other products which contain toxins, such as certain websites, electronic games, TV programs, films, magazines, books, and conversations. I will practice coming back to the present moment to be in touch with the refreshing, healing, and nourishing elements in me and around me, not letting regrets and sorrow drag me back into the past nor letting anxieties, fear, or craving pull me out of the present moment. I am determined not to try to cover up loneliness, anxiety, or other suffering by losing myself in consumption. I will contemplate interbeing and consume in a way that preserves peace, joy, and well-being in my body and consciousness, and in the collective body and consciousness of my family, my society, and the Earth.

This is the fifth of the Five Mindfulness Trainings. Have you made an effort to study, practice, and observe it during the past two weeks? (3 breaths)

[Bell]

Concluding Words

Brothers and Sisters, we have recited the Five Mindfulness Trainings, the foundation of happiness for the individual, the family, and society. We should recite them regularly so that our study and practice of the Mindfulness Trainings can deepen day by day.

Upon hearing the sound of the bell, please stand up and touch the Earth three times to show your gratitude to the Buddha, the Dharma, and the Sangha.

[Bell x3]

Ceremony to Transmit the Fourteen Mindfulness Trainings of the Order of Interbeing

All aspirants requesting to receive the Fourteen Mindfulness Trainings are seated in the central aisle of the hall facing the altar, with their Representative seated at the head of the group. The Representative may be a lay member of the Order of Interbeing, or one of the aspirants. The rest of the community is seated on either side, in rows, by age of ordination.

Sitting Meditation

12 minutes, preceded by instruction

Incense Offering

Touching of the Earth

Sutra Opening Verse

The Insight that Brings Us to the Other Shore

Formal Request

The Aspirants' Representative (with palms joined):
Namo Sakyamunaye Buddhaya.
Dear Respected Teacher, dear Noble Sangha, please listen to us with compassion. We [the list of the aspirants' names and Dharma names] would like to make a formal request.

[At the sound of the bell, the Representative and all the aspirants Touch the Earth one time. They then kneel with palms joined.]

The Aspirants' Representative makes the request in the name of all the aspirants:
Namo Sakyamunaye Buddhaya.
Dear Respected Teacher, dear Noble Sangha, we recognize that we're very fortunate. We have received a lot of merit from our blood ancestors and spiritual ancestors and, thanks to this, we have had the chance to receive and practice the Five Mindfulness Trainings.

The path of practice of the trainings has helped our love and understanding to grow, bringing transformation, healing and joy to ourselves and those around us. We have understood how valuable it is on this path to have a Sangha. Without the Sangha, how could we have been able to continue this beautiful practice in our daily life? If we flow with our Sangha as a river, we know we can reach the ocean of liberation. We would like to embrace the Sangha's career as our own.

In the past year, we have come together once a month to study the Fourteen Mindfulness Trainings. We have participated regularly in mindfulness days and retreats organized by our local Sangha or Plum Village. Today, with all our heart, we aspire to receive the Fourteen Precious Trainings of the Order of Interbeing. We understand clearly that following this path we are in the company of bodhisattvas, and that every moment can be a moment of happiness.

With our local Sangha's support, we humbly ask our dear spiritual ancestors and Noble Sangha to accept our request, and to transmit to us the Fourteen Trainings of the Order of Interbeing.

The Transmission Master replies:
We are happy to accept your request. You are very fortunate to have discovered such a wonderful path and to have the opportunity to commit yourselves to it. Your most beautiful task is to build a Sangha that can be a place of refuge for many people. This is what the Buddha did his whole life. Following this path you continue the Buddha's career. The Buddha and all the bodhisattvas will support you.

The Aspirants' Representative offers thanks:
We thank you dear Respected Teacher and dear Noble Sangha for accepting our request. We will follow your precious advice with all our heart.

[At the sound of the bell, the Representative and all the aspirants Touch the Earth twice more. If the Representative is not one of the aspirants, they then return to their place. All the aspirants remain in the center of the hall, and the ceremony begins.]

Sanghakarman Procedure

Sanghakarman Master: Has the entire community assembled?

Sangha Convener: The entire community has assembled.

Sanghakarman Master: Is there harmony in the community?

Sangha Convener: Yes, there is harmony.

Sanghakarman Master: Why has the community assembled today?

Sangha Convener: The community has assembled to perform the Sanghakarman of transmitting the Fourteen Mindfulness Trainings of the Order of Interbeing.

Sanghakarman Master: Noble community of Interbeing, please listen. Today, [date], has been chosen as the day to transmit the Fourteen Mindfulness Trainings of the Order of Interbeing. The community has assembled at the appointed time and is ready to transmit and receive the Fourteen Mindfulness Trainings in an atmosphere of harmony. Thus, the transmission can proceed. Such is the proposal. Is the proposal clear and complete?

Everyone: Clear and complete.

[Bell]

Bowing Deeply in Gratitude

On hearing the sound of the bell, after the recitation of each line, please touch the Earth one time.

In gratitude to your father and mother, who have brought you to life, please bow deeply before the Three Jewels in the Ten Directions.

[Bell]

In gratitude to your teachers, who have shown you how to understand and love, please bow deeply before the Three Jewels in the Ten Directions.

[Bell]

In gratitude to your friends, who give you guidance and support on the path, please bow deeply before the Three Jewels in the Ten Directions.

[Bell]

In gratitude to all beings in the animal, plant, and mineral worlds, please bow deeply before the Three Jewels in the Ten Directions.

[Bell x2]

Introductory Words

Today the community has gathered to give spiritual support to our brothers and sisters who will undertake to receive and observe the Fourteen Mindfulness Trainings of the Order of Interbeing and enter the core community of the Order of Interbeing.

Ordinees, please listen. Following in the steps of the bodhisattvas as your teachers and companions on the path, you have made the aspiration to receive and observe the Mindfulness Trainings of the Order of Interbeing. You have given rise to the seed of bodhicitta, the mind of love. You have made the aspiration to develop this seed. Your own awakening and liberation, as well as the liberation and awakening of all other species, have now become your highest career. Brothers and sisters in the community, please establish your mindfulness by enjoying your breathing, so that you may be truly present and give support to the seed of bodhicitta, the mind of love, in the ordinees. With your support, they will develop this seed solidly and courageously so that it will become indestructible.

Ordinees, this is the solemn moment for receiving the Fourteen Mindfulness Trainings of the Order of Interbeing. Listen carefully, with a clear and concentrated mind, to each mindfulness training as it is read, and answer, "Yes, I do" clearly every time you see that you have the intention and capacity to receive, study, and practice the mindfulness training that has been read.

Brothers and sisters, are you ready?
Ordinees: Yes, I am ready.

These, then, are the Fourteen Mindfulness Trainings of the Order of Interbeing.

Transmission of the Fourteen Mindfulness Trainings

The First Mindfulness Training
Openness

Aware of the suffering created by fanaticism and intolerance, we are determined not to be idolatrous about or bound to any doctrine, theory, or ideology, even Buddhist ones. We are committed to seeing the Buddhist teachings as a guiding means that help us learn to look deeply and develop understanding and compassion. They are not doctrines to fight, kill, or die for. We understand that fanaticism in its many forms is the result of perceiving things in a dualistic or discriminative manner. We will train ourselves to look at everything with openness and the insight of interbeing in order to transform dogmatism and violence in ourselves and the world.

This is the First Mindfulness Training of the Order of Interbeing. Do you make the commitment to receive, study, and practice it?
Ordinees: Yes, I do.

[Bell]

The Second Mindfulness Training
Nonattachment to Views

Aware of the suffering created by attachment to views and wrong perceptions, we are determined to avoid being narrow-minded and bound to present views. We are committed to learning and practicing nonattachment to views and being open to others' experiences and insights in order to benefit from the collective wisdom. Insight is revealed through the practice of compassionate listening, deep looking, and letting go of notions rather than through the accumulation of intellectual knowledge. We are aware that the knowledge we presently possess is not changeless, absolute truth. Truth is found in life and we will observe life within and around us in every moment, ready to learn throughout our lives.

This is the Second Mindfulness Training of the Order of Interbeing. Do you make the commitment to receive, study, and practice it?
Ordinees: Yes, I do

[Bell]

The Third Mindfulness Training
Freedom of Thought

Aware of the suffering brought about when we impose our views on others, we are determined not to force others, even our children, by any means whatsoever—such as authority, threat, money, propaganda, or indoctrination—to adopt our views. We are committed to respecting the right of others to be different, to choose what to believe and how to decide. We will, however, learn to help others let go of and transform fanaticism and narrowness through loving speech and compassionate dialogue.

This is the Third Mindfulness Training of the Order of Interbeing. Do you make the commitment to receive, study, and practice it?
Ordinees: Yes, I do

[Bell]

The Fourth Mindfulness Training
Awareness of Suffering

Aware that looking deeply at the nature of suffering can help us develop understanding and compassion, we are determined to come home to ourselves, to recognize, accept, embrace, and listen to our own suffering with the energy of mindfulness. We will do our best not to run away from our suffering or cover it up through consumption, but practice conscious breathing and walking to look deeply into the roots of our suffering. We know we can realize the path leading to the transformation of suffering only when we understand deeply the roots of suffering. Once we have understood our own suffering, we will be able to understand the suffering of others. We are committed to finding ways, including personal contact and using telephone, electronic, audiovisual, and other means, to be with those who suffer, so we can help them transform their suffering into compassion, peace, and joy.

This is the Fourth Mindfulness Training of the Order of Interbeing. Do you make the commitment to receive, study, and practice it?
Ordinees: Yes, I do.

[Bell]

The Fifth Mindfulness Training
Compassionate, Healthy Living

Aware that true happiness is rooted in peace, solidity, freedom, and compassion, we are determined not to accumulate wealth while millions are hungry and dying nor to take as the aim of our life fame, power, wealth, or sensual pleasure, which can bring much suffering and despair. We will practice looking deeply into how we nourish our body and mind with edible foods, sense impressions, volition, and consciousness. We are committed not to gamble or to use alcohol, drugs or any other products which bring toxins into our own and the collective body and consciousness such as certain websites, electronic games, music, TV programs, films, magazines, books, and conversations. We will consume in a way that preserves compassion, well-being, and joy in our bodies and consciousness and in the collective body and consciousness of our families, our society, and the Earth.

This is the Fifth Mindfulness Training of the Order of Interbeing. Do you make the commitment to receive, study, and practice it?
Ordinees: Yes, I do.

[Bell]

The Sixth Mindfulness Training
Taking Care of Anger

Aware that anger blocks communication and creates suffering, we are committed to taking care of the energy of anger when it arises, and to recognizing and transforming the seeds of anger that lie deep in our consciousness. When anger manifests, we are determined not to do or say anything, but to practice mindful breathing or mindful walking to acknowledge, embrace, and look deeply into our anger. We know that the roots of anger are not outside of ourselves but can be found in our wrong perceptions and lack of understanding of the suffering in ourselves and others. By contemplating impermanence, we will be able to look with the eyes of compassion at ourselves and at those we think are the cause of our anger, and to recognize the preciousness of our relationships. We will practice Right Diligence in order to nourish our capacity of understanding, love, joy and inclusiveness, gradually transforming our anger, violence, and fear, and helping others do the same.

This is the Sixth Mindfulness Training of the Order of Interbeing. Do you make the commitment to receive, study, and practice it?
Ordinees: Yes, I do.

[Bell]

The Seventh Mindfulness Training
Dwelling Happily in the Present Moment

Aware that life is available only in the present moment, we are committed to training ourselves to live deeply each moment of daily life. We will try not to lose ourselves in dispersion or be carried away by regrets about the past, worries about the future, or craving, anger, or jealousy in the present. We will practice mindful breathing to be aware of what is happening in the here and the now. We are determined to learn the art of mindful living by touching the wondrous, refreshing, and healing elements that are inside and around us, in all situations. In this way, we will be able to cultivate seeds of joy, peace, love, and understanding in ourselves, thus facilitating the work of transformation and healing in our consciousness. We are aware that real happiness depends primarily on our mental attitude and not on external conditions, and that we can live happily in the present moment simply by remembering that we already have more than enough conditions to be happy.

This is the Seventh Mindfulness Training of the Order of Interbeing. Do you make the commitment to receive, study, and practice it?
Ordinees: Yes, I do.

[Bell]

The Eighth Mindfulness Training
True Community and Communication

Aware that lack of communication always brings separation and suffering, we are committed to training ourselves in the practice of compassionate listening and loving speech. Knowing that true community is rooted in inclusiveness and in the concrete practice of the harmony of views, thinking, and speech, we will practice to share our understanding and experiences with members in our community in order to arrive at collective insight.

We are determined to learn to listen deeply without judging or reacting and refrain from uttering words that can create discord or cause the community to break. Whenever difficulties arise, we will remain in our Sangha and practice looking deeply into ourselves and others to recognize all the causes and conditions, including our own habit energies, that have brought about the difficulties. We will take responsibility for all the ways we may have contributed to the conflict and keep communication open. We will not behave as a victim but be active in finding ways to reconcile and resolve all conflicts, however small.

This is the Eighth Mindfulness Training of the Order of Interbeing. Do you make the commitment to receive, study, and practice it?
Ordinees: Yes, I do.

[Bell]

The Ninth Mindfulness Training
Truthful and Loving Speech

Aware that words can create happiness or suffering, we are committed to learning to speak truthfully, lovingly, and constructively. We will use only words that inspire joy, confidence, and hope as well as promote reconciliation and peace in ourselves and among other people. We will speak and listen in a way that can help ourselves and others to transform suffering and see the way out of difficult situations. We are determined not to say untruthful things for the sake of personal interest or to impress people, nor to utter words that might cause division or hatred. We will protect the happiness and harmony of our Sangha by refraining from speaking about the faults of other persons in their absence and always ask ourselves whether our perceptions are correct. We will speak only with the intention to understand and help transform the situation. We will not spread rumors nor criticize or condemn things of which we are not sure. We will do our best to speak out about situations of injustice, even when doing so may make difficulties for us or threaten our safety.

This is the Ninth Mindfulness Training of the Order of Interbeing. Do you make the commitment to receive, study, and practice it?
Ordinees: Yes, I do.

[Bell]

The Tenth Mindfulness Training
Protecting and Nourishing the Sangha

Aware that the essence and aim of a Sangha is the practice of understanding and compassion, we are determined not to use the Buddhist community for personal power or profit, or transform our community into a political instrument. As members of a spiritual community, we should nonetheless take a clear stand against oppression and injustice. We should strive to change the situation, without taking sides in a conflict. We are committed to learning to look with the eyes of interbeing and to see ourselves and others as cells in one Sangha body. As a true cell in the Sangha body, generating mindfulness, concentration, and insight to nourish ourselves and the whole community, each of us is at the same time a cell in the Buddha body. We will actively build brotherhood and sisterhood, flow as a river, and practice to develop the three real powers—understanding, love, and cutting through afflictions—to realize collective awakening.

This is the Tenth Mindfulness Training of the Order of Interbeing. Do you make the commitment to receive, study, and practice it?
Ordinees: Yes, I do.

[Bell]

The Eleventh Mindfulness Training
Right Livelihood

Aware that great violence and injustice have been done to our environment and society, we are committed not to live with a vocation that is harmful to humans and nature. We will do our best to select a livelihood that contributes to the well-being of all species on Earth and helps realize our ideal of understanding and compassion. Aware of economic, political, and social realities around the world, as well as our interrelationship with the ecosystem, we are determined to behave responsibly as consumers and as citizens. We will not invest in or purchase from companies that contribute to the depletion of natural resources, harm the Earth, or deprive others of their chance to live.

This is the Eleventh Mindfulness Training of the Order of Interbeing. Do you make the commitment to receive, study, and practice it?
Ordinees: Yes, I do.

[Bell]

The Twelfth Mindfulness Training
Reverence for Life

Aware that much suffering is caused by war and conflict, we are determined to cultivate nonviolence, compassion, and the insight of interbeing in our daily lives and promote peace education, mindful mediation, and reconciliation within families, communities, ethnic and religious groups, nations, and in the world. We are committed not to kill and not to let others kill. We will not support any act of killing in the world, in our thinking, or in our way of life. We will diligently practice deep looking with our Sangha to discover better ways to protect life, prevent war, and build peace.

This is the Twelfth Mindfulness Training of the Order of Interbeing. Do you make the commitment to receive, study, and practice it?
Ordinees: Yes, I do.

[Bell]

The Thirteenth Mindfulness Training
Generosity

Aware of the suffering caused by exploitation, social injustice, stealing, and oppression, we are committed to cultivating generosity in our way of thinking, speaking, and acting. We will practice loving kindness by working for the happiness of people, animals, plants, and minerals, and sharing our time, energy, and material resources with those who are in need. We are determined not to steal and not to possess anything that should belong to others. We will respect the property of others, but will try to prevent others from profiting from human suffering or the suffering of other beings.

This is the Thirteenth Mindfulness Training of the Order of Interbeing. Do you make the commitment to receive, study, and practice it?
Ordinees: Yes, I do.

[Bell]

The Fourteenth Mindfulness Training
True Love

For lay members: Aware that sexual desire is not love and that sexual relations motivated by craving cannot dissipate the feeling of loneliness but will create more suffering, frustration, and isolation, we are determined not to engage in sexual relations without mutual understanding, love, and a deep long-term commitment. We resolve to find spiritual support for the integrity of our relationships from family members, friends, and sangha with whom there is support and trust. We know that to preserve the happiness of ourselves and others, we must respect the rights and commitments of ourselves and others. Recognizing the diversity of human experience, we are committed not to discriminate against any form of gender identity or sexual orientation. Seeing that body and mind are interrelated, we are committed to learning appropriate ways to take care of our sexual energy and cultivating loving kindness, compassion, joy, and inclusiveness for our own happiness and the happiness of others. We must be aware of future suffering that may be caused by sexual relations. We will treat our bodies with compassion and respect. We are determined to look deeply into the Four Nutriments and learn ways to preserve and channel our vital energies (sexual, breath, spirit) for the realization of our bodhisattva ideal. We will do everything in our power to protect children from sexual abuse and to prevent couples and families from being broken by sexual misconduct. We will be fully aware of the responsibility of bringing new lives into the world and will meditate regularly upon their future environment.

For monastic members: Aware that the deep aspiration of a monk or a nun can only be realized when he or she wholly leaves behind the bonds of sensual love, we are committed to practicing chastity and to helping others protect themselves. We are aware that loneliness and suffering cannot be alleviated through a sexual relationship, but through practicing loving kindness, compassion, joy, and inclusiveness. We know that a sexual relationship will destroy our monastic life, will prevent us from realizing our ideal of serving living beings, and will harm others. We will learn appropriate ways to take care of our sexual energy. We are determined not to suppress or mistreat our body, or look upon our body as only an instrument, but will learn to handle our body with compassion and respect. We will look deeply into the Four Nutriments in order to preserve and channel our vital energies (sexual, breath, spirit) for the realization of our bodhisattva ideal.

This is the Fourteenth Mindfulness Training of the Order of Interbeing. Do you make the commitment to receive, study, and practice it?
Ordinees: Yes, I do.

[Bell]

Concluding Words

Brothers and sisters, you have received the Fourteen Mindfulness Trainings of the Order of Interbeing. You have taken the first step on the path of the bodhisattvas: the path of great understanding of Bodhisattva Manjusri that puts an end to countless wrong perceptions, prejudice, and discrimination; the path of great compassion of Bodhisattva Avalokitesvara, who loves, values, and protects the life of all species and listens deeply to the cries of all species far and near in order to help them; the path of great action of Bodhisattva Samantabhadra, who takes every opportunity to create love, understanding, and harmony in the world.

Brothers and sisters in the community, with one heart please give your spiritual support to the Ordinees in this present moment to help them now and in the future. Brothers and sisters, the Buddhas and bodhisattvas will be with you on your path of practice. When you hear the sound of the bell, please stand up and bow deeply three times to show your gratitude to the Three Jewels.

Transmission of Certificate of Ordination

Sharing the Merit

Concluding Words

Appendix

The Fourteen Precepts of the Order of Interbeing, 1987[26]

The First Precept

Do not be idolatrous about or bound to any doctrine, theory, or ideology, even Buddhist ones. All systems of thought are guiding means; they are not absolute truth.

The Second Precept

Do not think the knowledge you presently possess is changeless, absolute truth. Avoid being narrow-minded and bound to present views. Learn and practice nonattachment from views in order to be open to receive others' viewpoints. Truth is found in life and not merely in conceptual knowledge. Be ready to learn throughout your entire life and to observe reality in yourself and in the world at all times.

---

[26] From the first edition of *Interbeing*, Parallax Press, 1987.

The Third Precept

Do not force others, including children, by any means whatsoever, to adopt your views, whether by authority, threat, money, propaganda, or even education. However, through compassionate dialogue, help others renounce fanaticism and narrowness.

The Fourth Precept

Do not avoid contact with suffering or close your eyes before suffering. Do not lose awareness of the existence of suffering in the life of the world. Find ways to be with those who are suffering by all means, including personal contact and visits, images, sound. By such means, awaken yourself and others to the reality of suffering in the world.

The Fifth Precept

Do not accumulate wealth while millions are hungry. Do not take as the aim of your life fame, profit, wealth, or sensual pleasure. Live simply and share time, energy, and material resources with those who are in need.

The Sixth Precept

Do not maintain anger or hatred. As soon as anger and hatred arise, practice the meditation on compassion in order to deeply understand the persons who have caused anger and hatred. Learn to look at other beings with the eyes of compassion.

The Seventh Precept

Do not lose yourself in dispersion and in your surroundings. Learn to practice breathing in order to regain composure of body and mind, to practice mindfulness, and to develop concentration and understanding.

The Eighth Precept

Do not utter words that can create discord and cause the community to break. Make every effort to reconcile and resolve all conflicts, however small.

The Ninth Precept

Do not say untruthful things for the sake of personal interest or to impress people. Do not utter words that cause division and hatred. Do not spread news that you do not know to be certain. Do not criticize or condemn things that you are not sure of. Always speak truthfully and constructively. Have the courage to speak out about situations of injustice, even when doing so may threaten your own safety.

The Tenth Precept

Do not use the Buddhist community for personal gain or profit, or transform your community into a political party. A religious community, however, should take a clear stand against oppression and injustice and should strive to change the situation without engaging in partisan conflicts.

The Eleventh Precept

Do not live with a vocation that is harmful to humans and nature. Do not invest in companies that deprive others of their chance to live. Select a vocation which helps realize your ideal of compassion.

The Twelfth Precept

Do not kill. Do not let others kill. Find whatever means possible to protect life and to prevent war.

The Thirteenth Precept

Possess nothing that should belong to others. Respect the property of others, but prevent others from enriching themselves from human suffering or the suffering of other beings.

The Fourteenth Precept

Do not mistreat your body. Learn to handle it with respect. Do not look on your body as only an instrument. Preserve vital energies (sexual, breath, spirit) for the realization of the Way. Sexual expression should not happen without love and commitment. In sexual relationships, be aware of future suffering that may be caused. To preserve the happiness of others, respect the rights and commitments of others. Be fully aware of the responsibility of bringing new lives into the world. Meditate on the world into which you are bringing new beings.

Monastics and visitors practice the art of mindful living in the tradition of Thich Nhat Hanh at our mindfulness practice centers around the world. To reach any of these communities, or for information about how individuals, couples, and families can join in a retreat, please contact:

PLUM VILLAGE
33580 Dieulivol, France
plumvillage.org

LA MAISON DE L'INSPIR
77510 Villeneuve-sur-Bellot, France
maisondelinspir.org

HEALING SPRING MONASTERY
77510 Verdelot, France
healingspringmonastery.org

MAGNOLIA GROVE MONASTERY
Batesville, MS 38606, USA
magnoliagrovemonastery.org

BLUE CLIFF MONASTERY
Pine Bush, NY 12566, USA
bluecliffmonastery.org

DEER PARK MONASTERY
Escondido, CA 92026, USA
deerparkmonastery.org

EUROPEAN INSTITUTE OF APPLIED BUDDHISM
D-51545 Waldbröl, Germany
eiab.eu

THAILAND PLUM VILLAGE
Nakhon Ratchasima
30130 Thailand
thaiplumvillage.org

ASIAN INSTITUTE OF APPLIED BUDDHISM
Lantau Island, Hong Kong
pvfhk.org

STREAM ENTERING MONASTERY
Beaufort, Victoria 3373
Australia
nhapluu.org

MOUNTAIN SPRING MONASTERY
Bilpin, NSW 2758, Australia
mountainspringmonastery.org

For more information visit: *plumvillage.org*
To find an online sangha visit: *plumline.org*
For more resources, try the Plum Village app: *plumvillage.app*
Social media: *@thichnhathanh @plumvillagefrance*

PARALLAX PRESS, a nonprofit publisher founded by Zen Master Thich Nhat Hanh, publishes books and media on the art of mindful living and Engaged Buddhism. We are committed to offering teachings that help transform suffering and injustice. Our aspiration is to contribute to collective insight and awakening, bringing about a more joyful, healthy, and compassionate society.

View our entire library at **parallax.org**.

THE MINDFULNESS BELL, a Journal of the Art of Mindful Living in the Tradition of Thich Nhat Hanh, is published two times a year by Plum Village. To subscribe or to see the worldwide directory of Sanghas, visit **mindfulnessbell.org**.

THICH NHAT HANH FOUNDATION

planting seeds of Compassion

The Thich Nhat Hanh Foundation works to continue the mindful teachings and practice of Zen Master Thich Nhat Hanh, in order to foster peace and transform suffering in all people, animals, plants, and our planet. Through donations to the Foundation, thousands of generous supporters ensure the continuation of Plum Village practice centers and monastics around the world, bring transformative practices to those who otherwise would not be able to access them, support local mindfulness initiatives, and bring humanitarian relief to communities in crisis in Vietnam.

By becoming a supporter, you join many others who want to learn and share these life-changing practices of mindfulness, loving speech, deep listening, and compassion for oneself, each other, and the planet.

For more information on how you can help support mindfulness around the world, or to subscribe to the Foundation's monthly newsletter with teachings, news, and global retreats, **visit tnhf.org**.